TMH Professional: Cracking the IT Interview Series

Cracking the QTP Interview

Other Titles in this Series

- **Cracking IT Campus Interviews**
  Deepa Jain
- **Cracking the C, C++ and JAVA Interview, 2e**
  SG Ganesh and Subhash KU
- **Cracking the IT Interview, 2e**
  Balasubramaniam
- **Cracking the System Software Interview**
  Sandya Mannarswamy and SG Ganesh

TMH Professional: Cracking the IT Interview Series

Cracking the QTP Interview

Siva Koti Reddy. K

Sudhakar Kakunuri

Varaprasad. M

Tata McGraw Hill Education Private Limited
NEW DELHI

McGraw-Hill Offices

New Delhi New York St Louis San Francisco Auckland Bogotá Caracas
Kuala Lumpur Lisbon London Madrid Mexico City Milan Montreal
San Juan Santiago Singapore Sydney Tokyo Toronto

Tata McGraw-Hill

Published by Tata McGraw Hill Education Private Limited,
7 West Patel Nagar, New Delhi 110 008

Cracking the QTP Interview

ISBN (13): 978-0-07-133288-0
ISBN (10): 0-07-133288-X

Vice President and Managing Director: *Ajay Shukla*
Publishing Manager—Professional: *Praveen Tiwari*
Editorial Researcher—Science, Technology and Computing: *Sushil Gupta*
Sr. Copy Editor: *Neha Sharma*
DGM—Sales and Business Development—Professional: *S Girish*
Deputy Marketing Manager—Science, Technology and Computing: *Rekha Dhyani*
General Manager—Production: *Rajender P Ghansela*
Manager—Production: *Reji Kumar*

Typeset at Text-o-Graphics, B-1/56 Arawali Apartment, Sector 34, Noida 201 301 and
printed at Sanat Printers, EPIP, 312, HSIDC, Kundli, Sonepat, Haryana.

Cover Printer: Sanat Print

Cover Designer: Lets Think Simple

RALYCDRHRADYC

The McGraw·Hill Companies

To

All job seekers
who wish to crack their QTP interviews

Preface

A job interview is your chance to show an employer what kind of employee he or she will get if you're hired. That is why it is essential to be well prepared for the job interview. Job interviewing never seems to get any easier; even when you have gone on more interviews than you can count. You are meeting new people, selling yourself and your skills, and often getting the third degree about what you know or don't know. Knowledge is always your best weapon and so you should arm yourself with plenty of it. That starts with the very basic bit of knowledge regarding job interviews. Practice answering interview questions and practice your responses to the typical job interview questions and answers most employers ask. Think of actual examples you can use to describe your skills. Providing evidence of your successes is a great way to promote your candidacy.

Cracking the QTP Interview gives you the interview preparation you need to get the top software automation engineer jobs. If you're currently looking for a new job... If you've got an interview coming up soon... Or you've just never felt like you're making the best impression possible in past job interviews, then pay careful attention... This comprehensive book on QTP will help you ace your next job interview and finally crack the interview successfully. This book is for aspirants with varying profiles from fresher to mid-level experienced. This book sets out important guidelines on some implicit behavioral aspects of an interview which are usually under emphasized by aspirants. This book discusses all the aspects required to crack QTP automation interview starting from tool to covering hybrid automation framework with detailed focus on various aspects of Automation Scripting.

All the possible interview questions of a particular topic have been grouped in to a chapter with relevant title. This helps the reader to focus on interview questions of a particular topic where he or she has specific doubts thereby saving time to search a particular question. Answers are provided as if reader is in interview hall and facing the interviewer. This helps reader to feel and prepare the answers for questions by simulating his/her real world of interview.

Our heartfelt wishes for your great and rewarding career!!!

Siva Koti Reddy. K

Sudhakar Kakunuri

Varaprasad. M

Acknowledgements

No one walks alone on the journey of life. Just where you start to thank those who joined you, walked beside you, and helped you along the way continuously urged us to write a book, to put our thoughts down on over the years, those that we have met and worked with. So at last, here it is. So, perhaps this book and it's pages will be seen as "thanks" to the tens of thousands of you who have helped make our life what it is today.

We are very grateful to the editors for their continued hard work and commitment to this publication as well as to many advisers, without whose help this book could not have been compiled.

Siva Koti Reddy. K

Sudhakar Kakunuri

Varaprasad. M

Contents

CHAPTER 1

Automation Process

1. What are the Pros and Cons of Automation?

Pros:

- **Fast:** Automation Scripts run significantly faster than manual test execution
- **Reliable:** Tests perform precisely the same operations each time they are run, thereby eliminating human error
- **Repeatable:** One can test how the web site or application reacts, after repeated execution of the same operations
- **Programmable:** One can program sophisticated tests that bring out hidden information
- **Reusable:** One can re-use tests on different versions of a web site or application.

Cons:

- Everything cannot be automated. For Example: Look and Feel
- Automation cannot be applied for small projects since cost tends to be more as repetition is less
- Skilled resources are required for automation
- There are no tools available for automating applications which are developed with technologies like Multimedia.

2. How will you decide whether a particular scenario can be automated or not?

- ➢ Repetition of that scenario should be high
- ➢ Scenario should be functionally complete and stable
- ➢ GUI objects of scenario must be good for automation i.e., they must be identified by the automation tool.

3. Explain Different Testing Tools available.

- ➢ Functional Automation Test Tools
    - Quick Test Professional
    - WinRunner
    - SilkTest
    - Rational Functional Tester
    - Test Partner
    - Selenium
- ➢ Performance Test Tools
    - Load Runner
    - Silk Performer
    - Rational Performance Tester
    - WebLoad
    - Web Application Stress Tool (WAS)
    - OpenSTA
- ➢ Test Management Tools
    - Quality Center
    - QADirector
    - SilkCentral Test Manager
    - Rational Test Manager
    - QaTraq
    - Test Link
- ➢ Configuration Management Tools
    - VSS (Visual Source Safe)
    - CVS (Concurrent Version)
    - SVN (Sub Version)

   - SCCS(Source Code Control System)
   - Clear case
- ➢ Code Coverage Tools
   - GCov
   - JCov
   - Rational Pure Coverage
   - Optimizeit
   - Clover

4. Explain Automation Test Life Cycle, OR Explain Automation Test Methodology

Automation Test Life Cycle consists of three major phases- Planning, Design and Development and Execution.

Phase I : Automation Testing Planning

- ➢ Identification of Test Cases to Automate
- ➢ Decision for Automation Testing
- ➢ Acquisition of Automation Test Tool
- ➢ Setup and Training of Automation Testing Team

Phase II : Automation Testing Design and Development

- ➢ Design and Development of Automation Framework
- ➢ Development of Automation Test Scripts for each Test case to automate
- ➢ Review and Re-work of Test Scripts

Phase III : Automation Testing Execution

- ➢ Preparation of Automation Test Environment.
- ➢ Execution of Automation Test Scripts.
- ➢ Analysis of Test Results.

5. How can you decide whether a given project requires Automation or Not?

If a project has multiple releases, Automation is always beneficial, since in further releases you can use same scripts for regression. Even though multiple releases are not planned, it is always a good idea to automate regression tests, because we often run regression tests in maintenance phase.

6. What do you require to automate a given Testcase?

We just need Testcases which are documented step by step in detail and also the Test data to be used for running these Testcases.

7. How will you get the Testcases to Automate?

My team lead provides the list of Testcases to automate during the weekly project meeting. Usually I am supposed to automate 1-2 testcases per day. Based on the complexity and number of test steps involved, my lead will assign the number of testcases to automate in that particular week.

8. How will you get Test Data for Automation?

Test data is provided in Manual Testcases and we use the same for Parameterising in Automation.

9. Why do you run automated regression test scripts every week?

Our project is in maintenance phase and every week, bug fixes are happening. So, to ensure that there is no side effect, we run regression testcases on a weekly build.

10. How will you know when to execute Automated Testcases?

For every build, we execute the automated smoke and regression testcases. This is a continuous process.

11. During Execution, if Automated Testcase fails what will you do?

I will first analyze from the report as to which step has failed. I will run that test script alone again in a Debug mode. Sometimes, failures may be due to synchronization issues or also due to object identification issues. Since I am running in a debugging mode, I will be in a position to understand the exact failure. Sometimes I might realize that failure was not due to application; it was due to script error.

12. How do you know your automation script is correct?

After completion of writing the script I execute the scripts and check for functional flow testing. If it is working fine, I e-mail the lead, stating that the script is ready for Review. He then schedules a peer review with one or two colleagues for approval.

13. Do you conduct formal inspection on all the scripts developed?

No. We conduct only peer review for formal approval of Scripts.

14. How do the scripts of one release execute on another release?

I agree that GUI changes may be there in the next release, but 70% of the screen would remain same as that of the previous release. Even though 30% of the screens may have changed, changes are often in the form of new fields being added rather than deleting the existing fields. So old scripts will work 90% and we will do some minor changes to take care of any issues related to object identification.

15. As you mentioned you are already running the existing Automated Regression Testcases. Then what are you doing with Automation?

We have 200+ testcases to automate overall and we are done only with 60% as of now. Our project next version is due for release in next 3 months. We have an additional 80 testcases to automate newly; we also have to do significant enhancements to the existing testcases to work on the newer version. Overall, we have automation work for next 8 months in pipeline.

16. Do you need to know the application for doing Automation?

Though it is not compulsory; it is always a good idea to know the application for writing effective automation testcases. We usually execute the given testcases 2 times manually so as to closely observe how the application behaves and then we start with automation.

17. Can you automate the application without having its screens?

It is possible to write the scripts without application by understanding the objects of an application from SRS. However it is not a recommended approach, since lots of re-work will be involved after the availability of the actual application.

18. What is POC?

POC means Proof of Concept. This is useful in selecting an automation tool. This gives the perfect information about the tool, like what it can support when compared with other tools. The Automation Lead or an Automation Expert will be involved in preparation of POC, which will be created for multiple tools. POC will help the client in understanding ROI of automation efforts and also experience the advantages which automation brings, like Speed, Maximized coverage, etc.

CHAPTER 2

QTP First Look

1. How does QTP help in Automation?

QTP is a functional Automation Tool that is used to automate the functional tests of an Application Under Test (AUT)

2. Can I use QTP for Performance Testing?

No. Performance Testing can be conducted by another tool Load Runner from HP, who is also the provider of QTP. However, in Performance Testing, specific type of user called GUI VUser is created with QTP Script.

3. What is the latest version of QTP?

Latest Release is 11

4. Who is the provider of QTP?

HP

5. Can I automate Installation Testing using QTP?

Yes,you can, if installation package screens are developed with technologies supported by QTP.

6. What is the RAM and Hardisk Space required for installation of QTP?

RAM – 1GB

Hard Disk –1 GB of free disk space

7. What are the OS supported by QTP?

Windows XP

Win2K

Windows Vista

Win2003

Windows 7

8. Does a QTP support 64 bit OS?

Yes.

9. What are the Browsers supported by QTP

- Internet Explorer
- Firefox
- Chrome

10. List out the add ins supported by QTP

The following are the technologies that are supported by QTP 10.0

- Web
- Java(Core and Advanced)
- .Net
- WPF
- SAP
- Oracle
- Siebel
- PeopleSoft
- Delphi
- Power Builder

- Stingray1
- Terminal Emulator
- Flex
- Mainframe terminal emulators

11. What is the cost of QTP license?

I am sorry, I am not sure about the exact price. I heard it is around 9,000 USD.

Note: *As a test engineer it is not compulsory that you must know the licensing cost of the tool because it is usually procured by the client and shared with you.*

12. What is your team size?

12

13. How many licenses do you have?

4

14. When your team size is 12, how are you managing with 4 licenses?

Automation team size is only 6. 2 from US and 4 from India. Rest is Manual testing team.

15. How can 6 automation members manage with 4 licenses?

We use floating license. At any given point of time, 4 members can use QTP. If more than 4 are trying to open QTP, licensing server throws an error message. Since 2 of the team members are from US, we use the time difference effectively and share the licenses.

16. What are the different licenses supported by QTP

Three types of licenses are available for QTP from HP

- **Demo License:** This is a 30-day demo license. You can register and download QTP from HP site.
- **Seat License:** Seat License refers to assigning QTP to one machine. If we take 5 seat licenses QTP will be installed only in 5 computers and can be used only from these 5 computers.
- **Concurrent (Floating) License:** Concurrent License allows a license to be shared between machines at any given point in time. If we take 5 Concurrent licenses, QTP

can be installed in any number of computers. But only 5 users can login and use QTP at a time. License Server will be installed to monitor the number of users logged in.

If your company wants to automate and run test scripts with 4 members team, 2 in India and 2 in the US, it is better to opt for 2 concurrent licenses and use time zone difference effectively rather than having 4 Seat Licenses, though Cost of one Seat license is lower than cost of one Concurrent license.

CHAPTER 3

Record and Playback

1. What type of scripting technique do you follow? Recording & Playback or Scripting by using Object Repository or by using Descriptive Programming.

Do not say "We use Recording & Playback". Why because everybody expects the candidate must have good knowledge on scripting. So you can tell any of the remaining two.

2. Can you give me some scenarios where you have used Recording?

I have a situation where I need to work with some menu controls. I am unable to add the menu to object repository as it disappears when the mouse cursor is not on it. So, in that situation, I have used recording mechanism to add menu object to object repository.

Another scenario where I have used Recording is while working with right click operation in the application.

3. When do you use Analog Recording and Low Level Recording?

Analog Recording is to record mouse movements and Low level recording is useful for recording mouse coordinates. Low level Recording converts any object into win object and stores in the Object Repository.

4. What do you find in Expert View after recording a statement?

Expert View indicates a complete statement which represents an operation on the application. The object's class name, logical name, operation and data.

Window("IIBC").WinEdit("QTP").Set "Infics"

Here

Window and WinEdit are the class names

IIBC and QTP are the Logical Names

"Set" is an operation to insert the text

"Infics" is the data to enter in the edit box

5. What are the views/panes available in QTP?

1. Testpane
   a. Expert View
   b. Keyword View
2. Data table
3. Active Screen
4. Debug Viewer
5. Information
6. Missing Resources
7. To Do
8. Process Guidance
9. Test Flow
10. Available Keywords
11. Resources

6. What are the Toolbars available in QTP?

1. Standard : Useful to open, save and print Test
2. Automation : Useful to Record, Run and stop the Test
3. Debug : Useful to insert and remove a break point, to pause the test run and to do step by step executions
4. Edit : Useful to comment and uncomment, find and replace, undo and redo the statements
5. Insert : Useful to insert Checkpoints, Output Values, Actions and Transactions in a test

6. Tools : Useful to open Global settings, Object spy and to check syntax errors in test
7. View : Useful to View/Hide various panes in QTP IDE
8. Action : Useful to go to another action in the same test

Chapter 4

Object Identification

1. What is Logical Name and what is its role in QTP?

Logical name is a QTP defined name for a Test Object. The same name will be available in the script to refer to the test object in Object Repository. When you run, QTP searches for the test object in object repository which is specified in the script. If that test object name exists, then QTP will find the object in application.

Logical Name can be modified. If you modify the logical name in object repository, automatically that name will be replaced in the script where ever that object name exists.

2. What is a Test Object? How can we create it?

Test Object is an object created by QTP in the object repository, to refer to the original object in the application. A Test Object will have a set of properties which are copied from original object in application.

The Test Object can be created by Recording or by directly adding, by using Object Repository using add objects.

3. I have to prepare an Object Repository. But I don't have the application right now. How can I prepare?

In object Repository, there is an option to create an object manually (Object →Define New Test Object). In that, we have to specify the class and properties of that object.

Another solution is to prepare an XML Object Repository. There is a specific schema for creating object repository in XML.

4. When you run a script, How does QTP identify the objects in application?

When you run a script

Step1: QTP reads the statement and gets the Hierarchy, class and logical name

Step2: QTP searches for the same Hierarchy, class and logical name in Object Repository

Step3: If found in Object Repository, using the properties of that test object, QTP will try to find the object in application

Step4: If found in Application, QTP will perform the specified operation in script.

5. What is Physical Description or Object Description?

Physical/Object Description is a set of identification properties to identify the object in application. This will be created for every test object in Object Repository. This is the combination of Mandatory and Assistive Properties. These properties are pre-configured for every test object class in QTP.

6. What are the Object Identification types in QTP?

Normal Identification: Identifies the object using its description

Smart Identification: Identifies the object using smart configuration. But it will be used only in case of failure of normal identification and if it is already configured and activated.

Ordinal Identifiers: Identifies based on index and location of the object.

7. How do you modify the properties of an object during Run Session?

Manually we cannot modify the properties during run session. We can do this by using setTOproperty method. This method is available for all test object classes.

8. What are the Object Repository types and what is the extension?

Two types Object Repositories are :

1. Local
2. Shared

The Extension for Local is ".BDB"

The Extension for Shared is ".TSR"

9. When do you use Local and Shared Repositories?

Local Repository is suggested when the application has very few tests to develop and there are no frequent changes. It is also useful in building the single action tests.

Shared Repository is suggested if we need to update/modify object properties on a regular basis and when developing multi action tests which are having called actions.

10. How do you prepare an Object Repository?

Object Repository creation follows steps as below:

a. Identify Modules and Controls to be tested in the Application
b. Configure Object Identification Properties for each control class
c. Add all Objects to Object Repository module by module
d. Remove unnecessary objects and give appropriate name to existing objects if required
e. Move the repeated objects like "Save", "Yes" and "No" buttons under a global module

11. What is the difference between Identification Properties and Native Properties?

An object in the application may have lot of properties assigned to it when developing. Those properties are called as native properties. But QTP takes very few properties especially for identification purpose. These properties are called as Identification properties. We can observe this Native and Identification properties list in Object Spy window.

12. What is the Test Architecture of QTP?

- A Test consists of call of actions
- Actions help Tests divide the test into logical units
- Each Action consists of steps, Data Table, Local Object Repository and Associated Shared Object Repositories
- The Test can have Library files, Environment Files, Recovery Scenarios associated with it.

13. When you add an object from web application it shows as Win Object. What may be the problem?

If a web application is identified as Win Object, there could be multiple reasons behind it:

1. Web addin not selected
2. The Browser is opened before opening QTP
3. If we have selected "Do not Record and Run on Browsers that are already open" option in Record and Run settings
4. The Browser is not supported by QTP

14. I have added a Text Area from web application. But it is added as web element. Why has this problem occurred and how to overcome it?

If any object is not added by using its standard class, which means the object class is not available in QTP Test Object Classes list. Even though it is displayed as a Text Area in Application, the developers might have used a different technology to create it.

In this situation, we have to find the technology they used and get that add-in to work with. If not, we have to use DOM methods or sendkeys method or Mercury Devise Replay Object to enter the text in text area.

Example for this type of object: Gmail/Yahoo compose mail body area

15. I have added a Text Box from Windows application. But it is added as Win Object. Why has this problem occurred and how to overcome it?

If any object is not added by using its standard class, which means the object class is not available in QTP Test Object Classes list. For windows application, there is a facility to map custom class to standard class. All that you need to do is, add that Text box object class in to custom class list and map it to winedit class. Whenever you add that object automatically it will add as winedit object.

16. How do you Add/Modify object properties of a shared repository when it is used by your team?

Every project maintains a shared location to store all the Project Data. In the same way the Object repositories are also kept in a shared location and will be accessible for all the team members. If we have write permissions, we can directly open the object repository from QTP for modifying it. The changes will be reflected automatically for others.

17. How do you associate one shared object repository for all the actions available in the test?

If we go to Object Repository window → Tools → Associate Repositories, a new window opens that enables to add Shared Object Repository. We can add a Repository and we can associate that repository to all available actions in the same window.

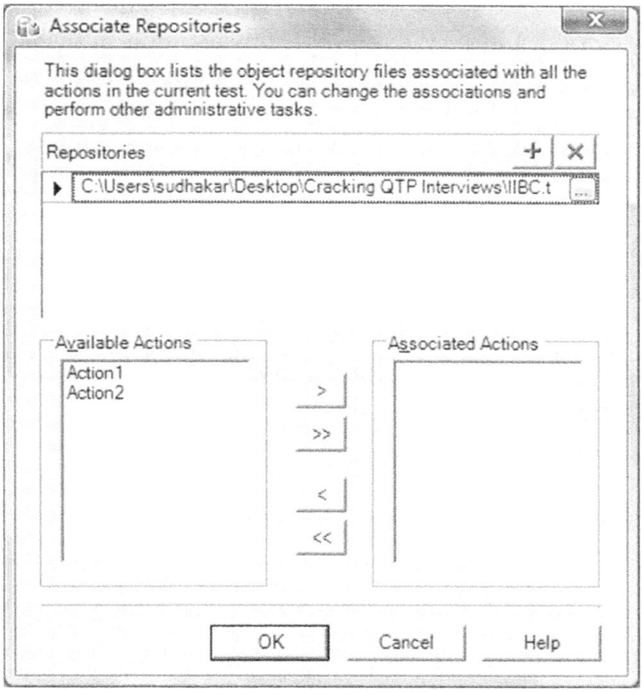

18. How can you give your object identification settings to other team members?

Object Identification Settings are very important to make sure that all the team members are using same type of identification settings. To make those settings, initially one person in the team should configure all the properties manually in Tools → Object Identification window and Clicks on Generate Script Button. This will generate a script which has Configured Object Identification Settings. This file will be shared to all other team members. To load the settings just double click on that VBS File.

19. How do you load Object Repository in runtime?

We can load Object Repositories in run time using Repositories Collection utility Object.

Syntax:

RepositoriesCollection.Add(RepPath)

20. What is the difference between Mandatory and Assistive Properties?

Mandatory and Assistive properties are the preconfigured properties in QTP object identification settings. These are useful to create a unique description for a Test Object. Whatever are the properties available in Mandatory properties list, all of them should get added to Object description and if those properties are not sufficient to create the unique description, then QTP adds one by one, the assistive property to create a unique description.

Ex: Assume that 5 mandatory and 3 assistive properties are available for an object. If you add that object, all 5 mandatory properties will get added mandatorily. If QTP feels that the object is not having a unique description, then the Assistive properties will get added one by one to those 5 properties. If the object gets the unique description at first property, then the Object Description will have 5 Mandatory + 1 Assistive properties.

21. What is the difference between Normal and Smart Identification Types?

If QTP identifies an object only by using Object description which is added in Object Repository then that is called as Normal Identification.

When Normal Identification fails to identify the object and smart identification is activated then QTP uses Smart Identification.

Smart Identification uses two sets of properties called base filter properties and optional filter properties to identify the object.

In Normal Identification, all the properties will be used to identify the object at the same time and because of this, if any one property fails, the object is not identifiable.

Ex: If an object has 5 properties in object description, when identifying the object, all 5 properties should be satisfied. Even if one property fails, QTP doesn't identify the object.

In Smart Identification, if one property fails, it uses another property to identify the object. Considering the above scenario, if one property fails in available 5 properties, it uses remaining 4 properties to identify the object.

22. What is the difference between Index and Location?

Index: - The tab index of the object in application. The first created object will have index 0.
Location: - The object position based on X, Y co-ordinates in the application.

23. What is creation time and in which situations can we use it?

Creation time is an ordinal identifier which is only available for Browser Test Object Class. After opening QTP, the first opened browser will have creation time "0". The next opened browser will have the creation time "1". If you close the first browser, the second opened browser will get "creation time 0". We can use this if the browser title is dynamic. Most of the people use this in descriptive programming.

24. What are the resources of a QTP Test?

A Resource is a file which helps QTP in developing and execution of a Test. The resources are

- Object Repositories
- Function Libraries
- Internal and External Actions
- Recovery Scenarios
- Data tables
- Environment Files
- Virtual Object Files

25. What is the difference between Object Repository window and Object Repository Manager?

Object Repository window is available for every Action. This will have a local repository and associated shared object repositories. We can create shared object repositories by exporting local repository. But we cannot do any modifications to shared repository.

Object Repository Manager is to create, modify and merge shared object repositories. We can export/import shared object repositories to/from xml files.

26. When do you go for Merging of Object Repositories?

Merging is useful for easy maintenance of Object Repositories. You might have developed multiple Object repositories for your application and later identified that you have repeated objects in your repositories. This leads to more maintenance. In order to remove the repentance of object, we go for merging. Generally, maintaining single repository is easier than maintaining multiple repositories.

In a project, not everybody will have the permission to modify the shared object repository. Generally, one person in the team maintains the shared object repository. This is useful to ensure that the objects added by one person are not getting modified or added again by another person. In this situation if any team member wants to add any objects to repository, they will add the objects to local repository and at the end of the day they will send it to the person who is doing the maintenance activity. He will merge those repositories with existing shared repository and make it available as updated repository to all.

27. How many Repositories can be merged at a time in QTP?

In QTP we can merge only two repositories at a time.

28. Can we merge Local Repository (.BDB) and Shared Repository, Local Repository and Local Repository?

Yes. We can merge Shared Repository with Local and Local Repository with Local.

29. What are the ways to store objects in QTP?

We can store objects in Local and Shared Object Repositories. Apart from this we can store objects in XML files.

30. What is the use of creating XML Object Repositories?

Object Repositories are opened only by QTP. You cannot read/edit them outside of QTP. If you store objects in XML, you can read/modify the object properties without opening QTP. To edit object repositories, we must know about XML and QTP Object Repository Schema.

31. How can you find if a Test Object has captured the correct properties of an Object?

After adding the object to repository, to ensure that it captures unique properties or not, we have to highlight the object. If the added object is highlighted in application, then the object is added with unique properties.

32. When I added some objects to repository, the logical names that QTP assigned is like Button_1, Button_2, and Button_3. Why has this happened?

This happens if those buttons do not have any titles on them. By default, QTP is configured for all the objects whose property should be considered as logical name. In the same way for button, Text property is the logical name. If that text is not available on the button, next priority goes to class name. If the application is having multiple buttons with no text on it, then those buttons will be captured as Button_1, Button_2, and Button_3.

33. In the above scenario based on the button functionality, I want to rename the objects in repository. But I don't know what button is for which purpose. How can I rename the Objects?

If the objects are added like Button_1, Button_2, and Button_3, we have to rename the objects based on the object functionality. To identify which button is for which functionality, we have to highlight each object in application and modify the name based on observation.

34. How can you specify an object repository, which can be added in subsequent created Actions in a Test?

This we have to do in initial stages of the script development. In QTP Testing process, creation of resources is the second step. Creation of resources includes Object Repository also. When developing a Test, it should start with Action1. If we are going to create multiple actions in the test we might need to have shared repository associated with all Actions. To automatically associate a shared repository to all subsequent actions, we have to go Edit → Action → Action Properties → In Associated Repositories Tab → Add a Repository and Click on "Set As Default" button.

Below is the Actions properties Screen

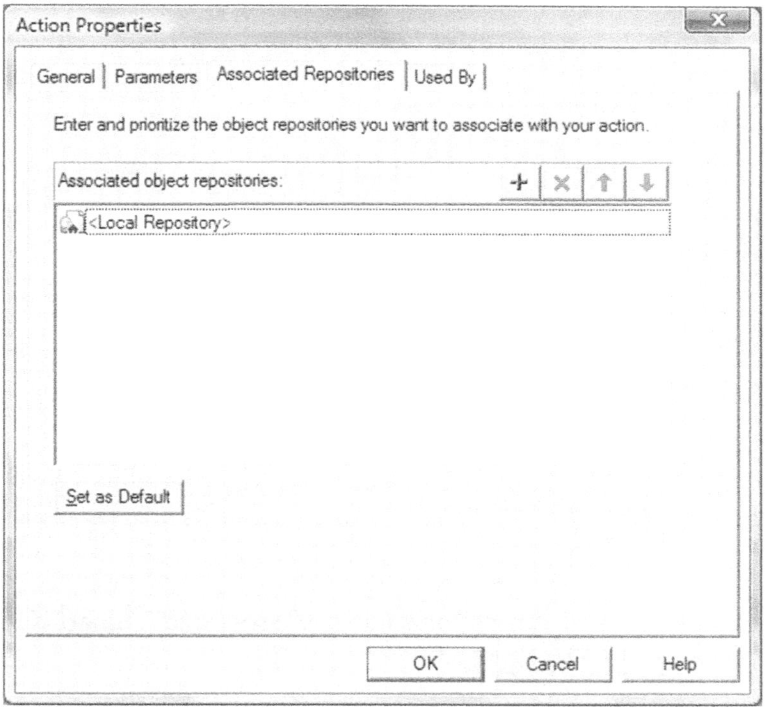

35. When you prepare an Object Repository, How can you add only specific type of objects?

In Object Repository using "Add Objects" option, we can add all objects from the application, based on the selected object. If we are adding a parent level object, QTP asks us whether to add all of its child objects. In that, we can select only the object type which we want. If you want only buttons to be added in object repository, then you select only button checkbox and click on ok. All button objects will get added.

EX: If you select a page object using add objects option, it displays below screen (Define Object Filter). In that, we can configure specific object types to add by clicking selected object type. The below screen (Select Object Types) provides a facility to filter specific type of objects.

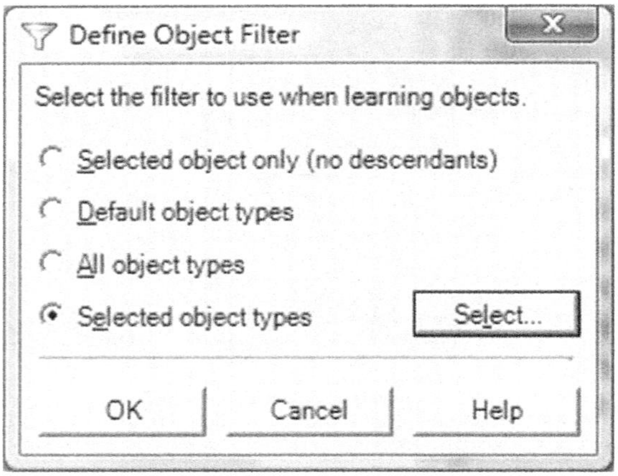

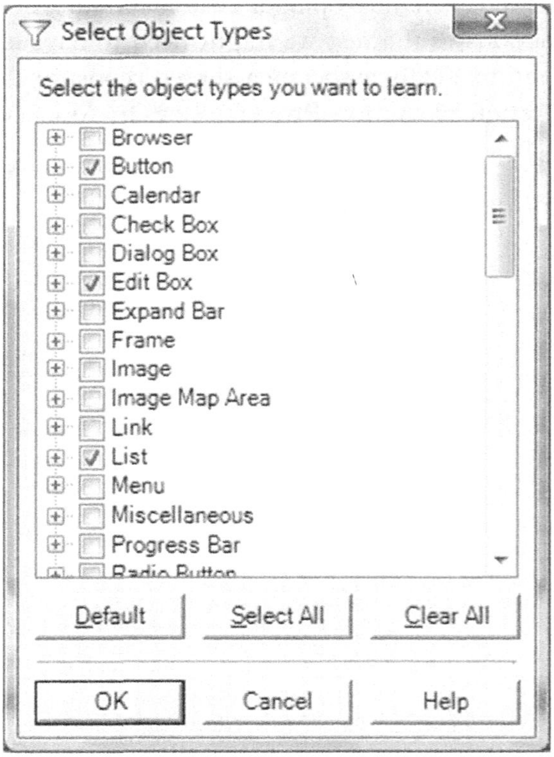

36. I have an object in Local Repository and in Associated Shared Repository. Which Repository object does QTP consider?

QTP always considers object from Local Repository if that object exists. If object does not exist in local repository then, QTP goes to the next specified shared repository.

We can set the shared object repository priority in Action Properties dialog. In the below Action Properties dialog,there are two shared repositories specified and by default local repository is available. Based on the below priority, QTP searches for the object in local repository, if the object does not exist in local, then QTP searches for the object in next specified Shared Object Repository IIBC.tsr.

We can change the Shared Object repositories priority by using Top and Down arrows. But we can't change the position of Local Repository.

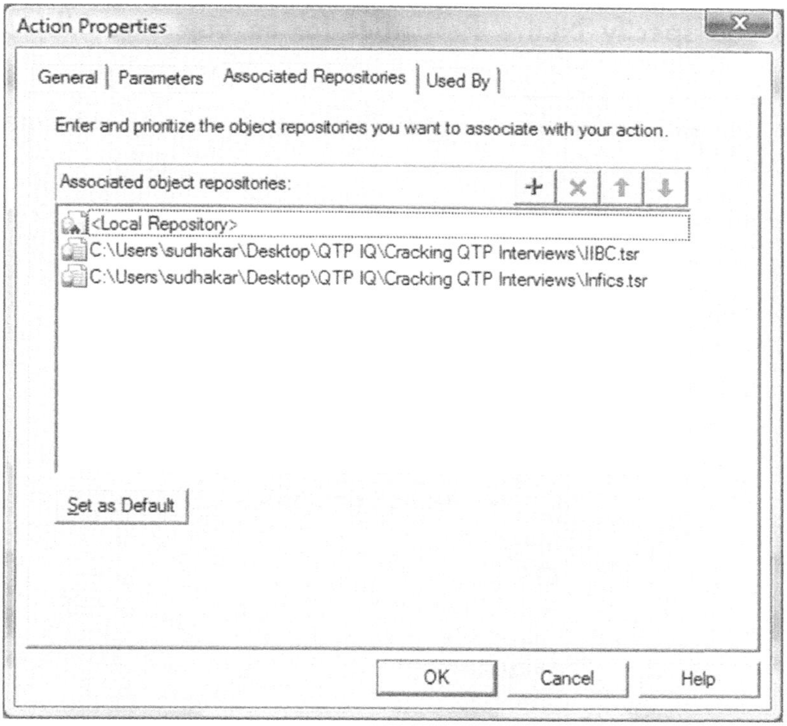

37. What is the size of an Object Repository?

There is no size limitation for Object Repository.

38. We have lot of modules in our application. There are different teams who haveworked for each module. Every team has prepared their own object repository. Now the modules

are completely integrated hence the flow of scripts is extended to other modules. How can we use object repositories in this scenario?

Object Repository merging is the solution. Merge all repositories into one repository and make use of that repository for all scripts. Even if script flow is increased to other modules, the same repository will be useful for all scripts.

39. Explain Object Spy?

Object Spy is to show the information about the object. The information includes Identification Properties, Native Properties, Test Object Operations and Native Methods.

40. How do you specify Native Properties for an object in Object Identification window?

We can configure a new property as an identification property in Object Identification window. To configure that

Go to Tools → Object Identification window → Select Web Environment →under Mandatory properties list, click on Add/Remove

A new window opens which a list of properties has specified.

Any defined property will get added in this list. To define a property click on new. New Property dialog opens.

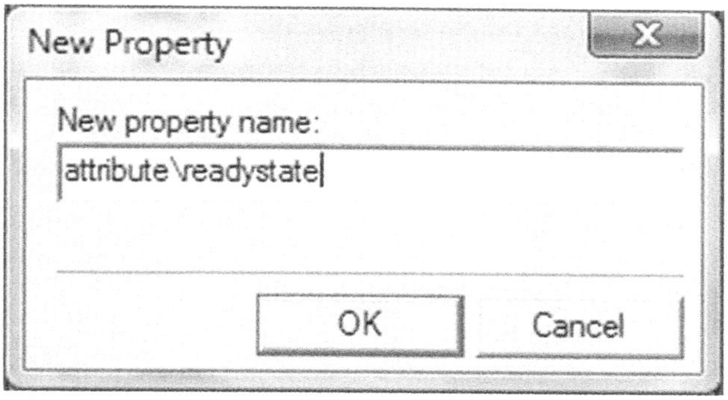

In the above dialog enter "Attribute/property name". Automatically whenever an object is added from that class, the object will have the configured property with value. When you spy on the object, the property will be displayed in Identification Properties list.

41. Explain Smart Identification.

Smart Identification is an advanced identification mechanism to identify the objects in application in case of failure of normal identification. This will be used by QTP only in Script Runtime.

Smart Identification has two types of properties.

Base Filter Properties: These are basic properties like class, html tag...etc. These properties are used to create a main list of objects which has basic properties match.

Optional Filter Properties: This will have regular identification properties like name, value, text...etc. These are used to filter the main list created by Base Filer Properties.

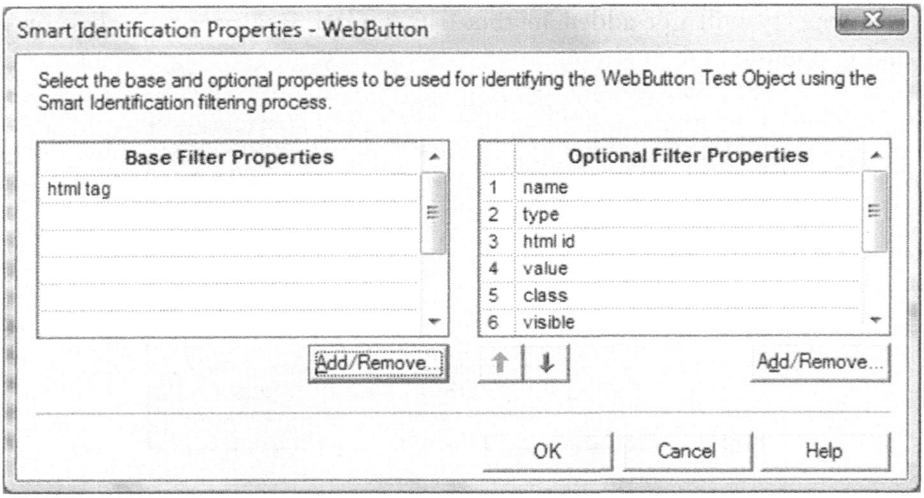

The above diagram shows the smart identification configuration of Web Button. Assume that the Property values are specified as below:

Html tag : Input

Name : Save

Type : Button

Html Id : button1

Value : Save

If normal identification fails, then Smart Identification will be activated and first it prepares a list "Input" html tag objects using base filter properties. Assume that it has found 15 Input tag objects.

These 15 objects will get filtered by one by one optional filter properties.

In that 15 objects list how many are having name property as "Save". Similarly, all properties will look for a match until it reaches 1 filtered object.

If one object is filtered by 1st optional filter property, then all other properties will get ignored.

If no object is filtered by 1st optional filter property, then the property will get skipped and QTP goes for next property to filter the objects.

42. How can you disable smart identification for a single Object?

In Object Repository, go to the object for which you want to disable smart identification, In Test Object details section, go to "Additional Details" and make it false at enable smart identification.

Below window shows where to disable smart identification.

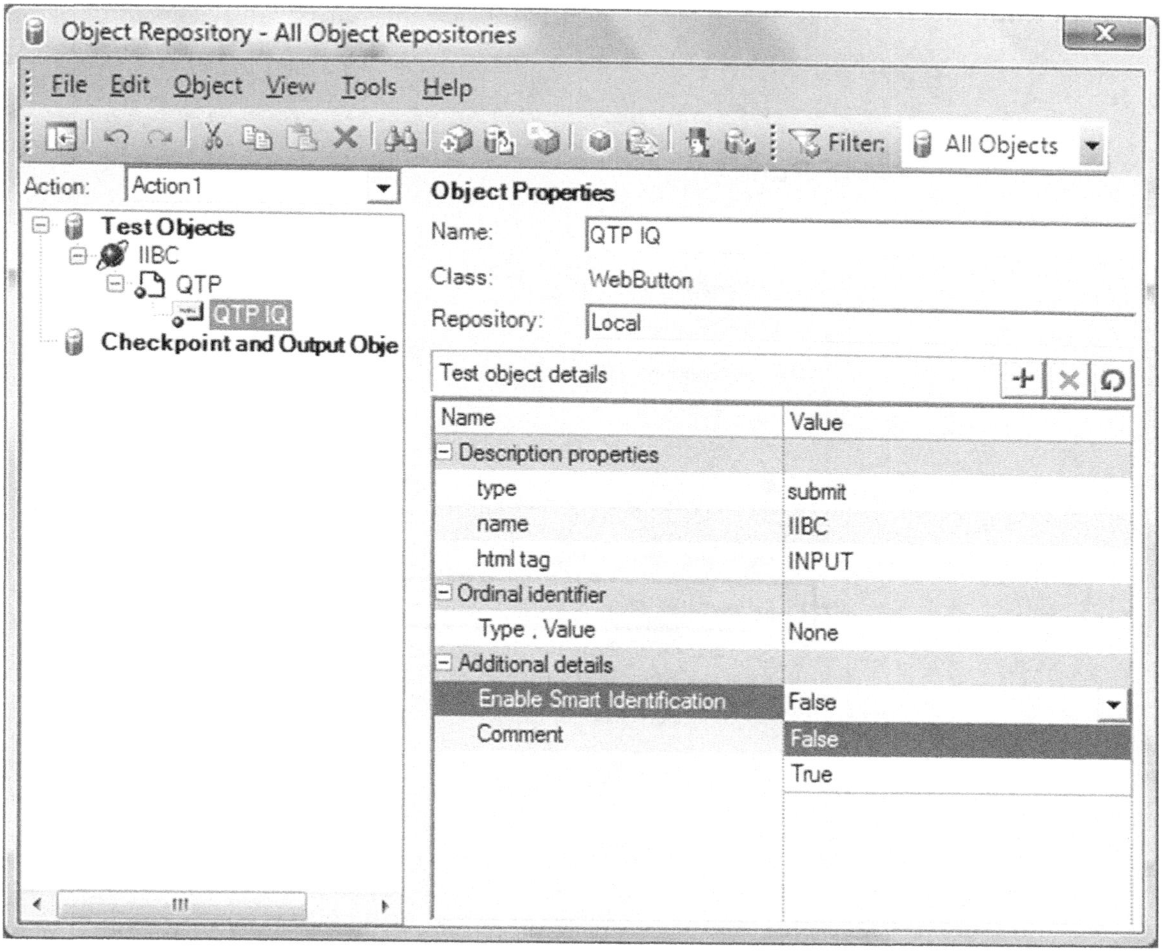

43. When you add an object in to repository, it is added with an Index number. What is the meaning of that?

That means there are multiple objects which have the same properties. If there are two save buttons on the page, when you add an object, that object will get added with an index number to uniquely identify the object.

44. How can you disable smart identification for all Objects?

We can disable smart identification in File →settings→ Run → Select the checkbox "Disable Smart Identification During Run Session"

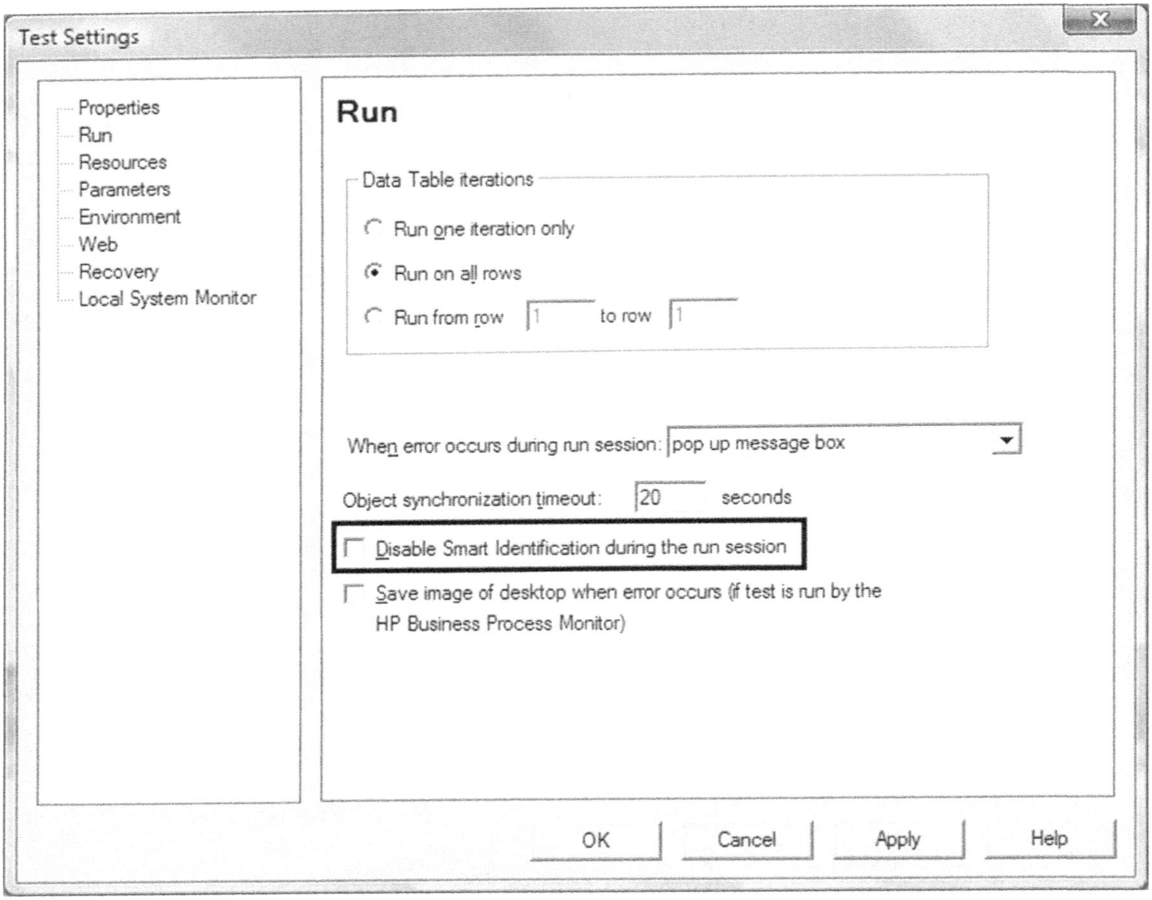

CHAPTER 5

Actions

1. What is an Action?

Action is a logical unit of the Test. An action consists of its own test script, including all of the steps in that action, Data table and any objects in its local object repository.

2. How many Actions can be created in a Test?

We can create n number of Actions in a test. But only 255 actions will have the data tables.

3. What are the resources of an Action?

By default, every action will have Script, Data table and Local object repository. Apart from that if you associate any shared object repositories, those also will become the resources of Action.

4. What are types of Actions?

There are 3 types of Actions

Non-Reusable/Normal Actions: A non-reusable action is the one which cannot be called by any other actions and can be called only once within the test it is created.

Reusable Actions: A reusable action is the one which can be called by any other actions and can be called multiple times from any other actions.

External Actions: A reusable action stored with another test. External actions are read-only in the calling test, but you can choose to use a local, editable copy of the Data Table information for the external action.

5. What are the types in splitting Actions?

An action can split in two ways

Independent Splitting: The Action splits in to two different and independent actions.

Nested Splitting: The Action splits in to interlinked actions, a parent action and a child action will be created. If you execute the parent action, automatically child action will get executed.

6. How can you call a Reusable Action in Current Test?

We can call a Reusable action by using call to existing action option or by using a scripting statement.

1st Method:
Go to Insert → Call to Existing Action → Select the Action from Actions list → Click on OK

2nd Method:
Use Run action "Action Name", Iterations Statement to call the reusable action.

7. How can you call a Reusable Action in Other Test?

We can call a Reusable action by using call to existing action option or by using a scripting statement.

1st Method:
Go to Insert → Call to Existing Action → Select the Test using browse button → Select the Action from Actions list → Click on OK

2nd Method:
Use Load And Run action "Test Path","Action Name", Iterations Statement to call the reusable action in other tests.

8. What is an External Action?

A Reusable Action which is stored with another test and is called in current Test.

9. How to load the Action in Runtime?

Use LoadAndRunAction "Test Path","ActionName",Iterations to load the action in runtime.

10. If you call an Action from One Test to Another, What are the resources that can be used in other Test?

If you call an action from another test, all the action resources like script, Local Repository, associated shared repositories and data table will be used in other test.

11. If you save a test, you can identify a folder called "Action0" in test path. What is the role of Action0?

Action0 have the calls of all other actions in the test. It is not displayed in QTP IDE, but it is playing a very important role in QTP test by calling all the actions.

12. What is Default Action type?

Up to QTP 9.2 by default the Action is Non-Reusable Action. From QTP 9.5 the default Action type is Reusable Action.

13. I want to make an Action Non Reusable. But the Reusable Checkbox is in disable state. What is the reason?

We cannot make an action non-reusable if that is already called by other actions.

14. What are the conditions to call an Action from Another?

The source action must be a reusable action.

15. What is Action Template?

Action Template is to include one or more statements in every new action created in the test. For example, if you always enter your name as the author of an action, you can add this comment line to your action template. An action template applies only to actions created on your computer.

16. How do you configure Action Template?

Create a text file containing the comments, function calls, and other statements that you want to include in your action template. The text file must be in the structure and format used in the Expert View. Save the text file as ActionTemplate.mst in your <QuickTest Installation Folder>\dat folder. All new actions you create contain the script lines from the action template.

Note: Only the file name ActionTemplate.mst is recognized as an action template.

CHAPTER 6

CheckPoints

1. How do you use checkpoints in your project?

We are using customized function to verify the objects. We have created some generic verification functions using GetROproperty and CheckProperty methods to check the object properties.

Sample Function

```
Function VerifyPropertyValue(vObject,vObjProperty,vObjExpectedValue)

      VerifyPropertyValue=vObject.CheckProperty (vObjProperty,vObjExpect
      edValue)

End Function
```

2. What are the different types of CheckPoints in QTP?

- Standard Checkpoint
  - Page Checkpoint
  - Image Checkpoint
  - Table Checkpoint
- Text Checkpoint
- Text Area Checkpoint
- Bitmap Checkpoint

- ➢ Database Checkpoint
- ➢ Accessibility Checkpoint
- ➢ XML Checkpoint (From Application)
- ➢ XML Checkpoint (From Resource)

3. Where does CheckPoint store its information?

Checkpoint stores its information in Object Repository.

4. For what type of CheckPoints is the recording mandatory?

Recording is mandatory for the checkpoints which are to work with GUI objects. Database and XML Checkpoint from Resource is not related with Application GUI. So to insert these check points, recording is not mandatory. For all remaining checkpoints, recording is mandatory because we have to show an object from the Application.

5. Which CheckPoint is used for checking properties of an object?

Standard checkpoint is used to check properties of an object.

6. I have to verify the text on web element. Which CheckPoint can I use?

We can use Standard and Text checkpoints to verify the text on web element. To use standard checkpoint, we have to select "outertext" property of the object.

7. What is the statement to be used to check a single property for an object?

```
Object Hierarchy.CheckProperty PropertyName,PropertyValue,Timeout
```

8. How does a CheckPoint work in QTP?

When inserting a check point, QTP automatically captures the expected values of the properties. These values will be verified in runtime. A Checkpoint compares the Actual Value to the Expected Value.

9. For what type of checkpoints, Parameterization is not possible?

For Bitmap and Accessibility Checkpoints parameterization is not possible. Because there is no bitmap data holder in QTP like it has for text.

Accessibility checkpoint is specially for checking WebStandards. Those standards are defined by W3C. Hence we cannot parameterize.

10. What is the difference between Text and Text Area CheckPoints?

Text Checkpoint is to check the text on an object. This can be applied on multiple environments.

Text Area Checkpoint is to check specific area text of the object. This can be applied only on windows applications.

11. What is the difference between Bitmap and Image CheckPoints?

Bitmap Checkpoint is to check the appearance of the Bitmap.

Image Checkpoint is to check the properties of an image. This can be created by inserting standard checkpoint on an Image object.

12. What are hidden checkpoints in QTP and how can we use them?

Page, Image and Table check points are hidden check points in QTP. We can use those checkpoints only by inserting standard checkpoint on page, image and table objects. Page and Image checkpoints support only Web Add in environments. Table Checkpoint supports all GUI environments.

13. What is Accessibility Checkpoint and where do you configure it?

Accessibility Checkpoint is to check Standards of the Web Page according to the W3C Web Content Accessibility Guidelines. For example, guideline 1.1 of the W3C Web Content Accessibility Guidelines requires you to provide a text equivalent for every non-text element. You can add an Alt property check to check whether objects that require the Alt property under this guideline, do in fact have this tag.

The Accessibility Checkpoint configuration should be done at QTP global web advanced options.

Go to Tools → Options → Web → Advanced → Accessibility Checkpoint

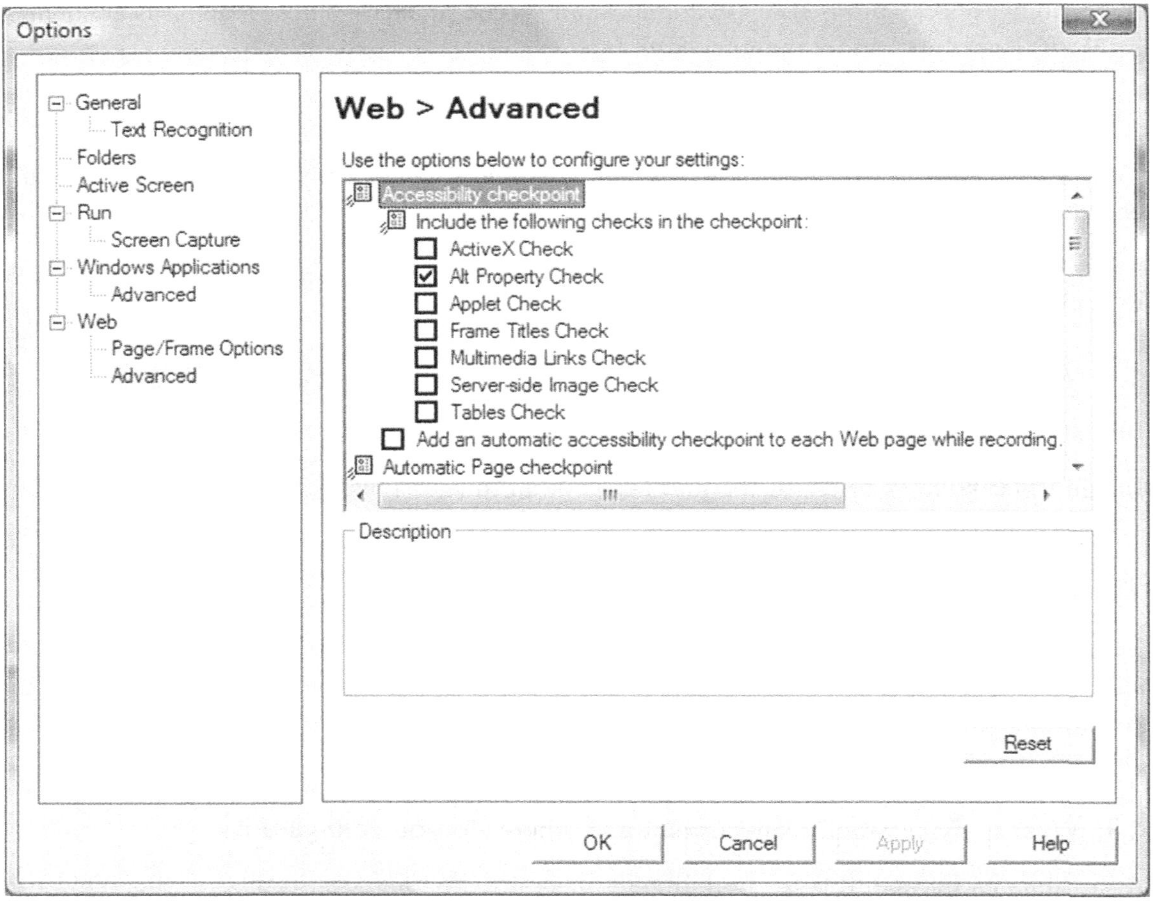

Configurations and Modification for the Accessibility checkpoint should be done at only this place.

14. How can you test a Scenario for which the text should not display on an object/area?

We can use Text check point for this scenario. There is an option "Text not displayed" in Text checkpoint to check Text should not display on object/area. If this option is selected, QTP checks for the selected text should not display on the specified object/area.

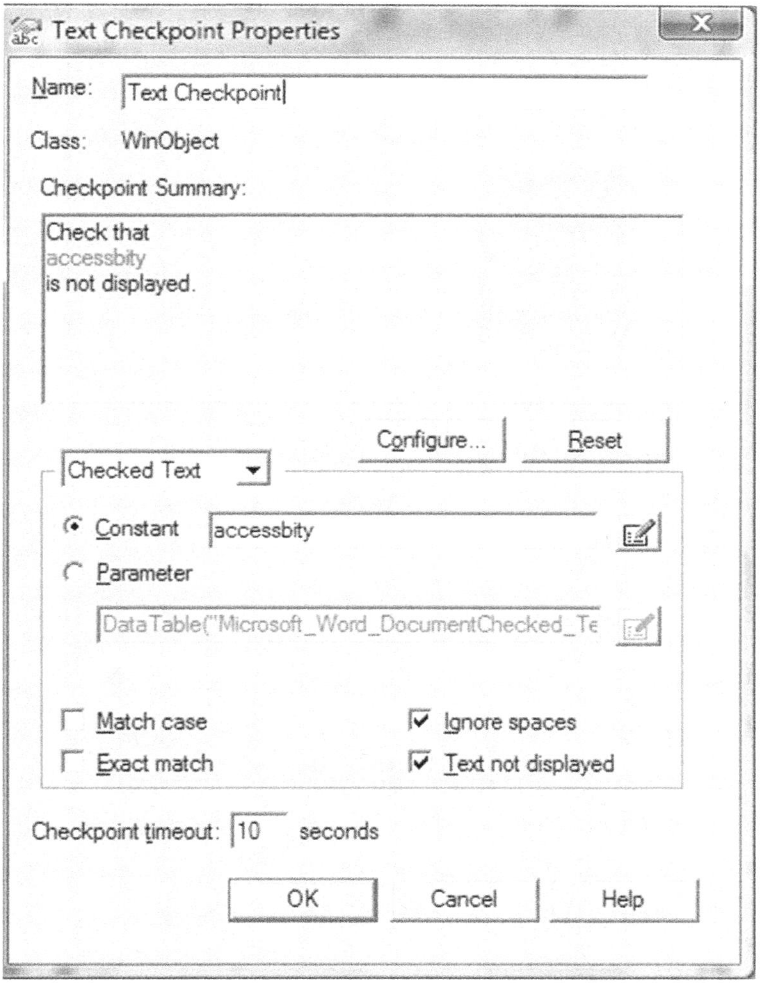

15. I want to verify only first row data in the Database. What is the configuration that I need to follow?

To verify only first row data in the database, you need to configure Database checkpoint. When you insert database checkpoint, QTP displays a wizard called Database Query Wizard. Select "Maximum Number of Rows" checkbox and give how many rows you want to test in DB. QTP will fetch only that specified number of row values.

Another method is, get all the data by using select queries and select only first row in the query data.

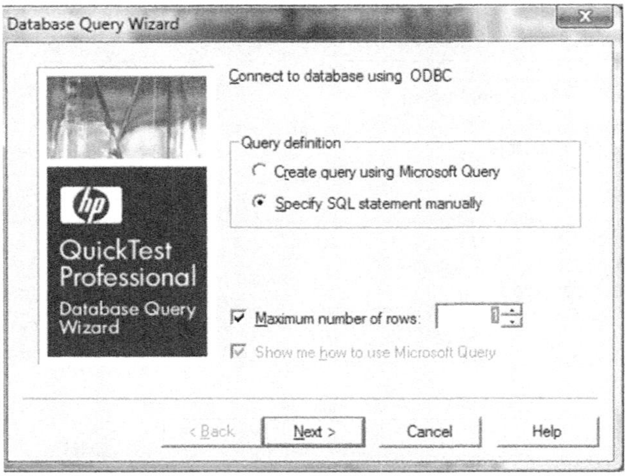

1st Method

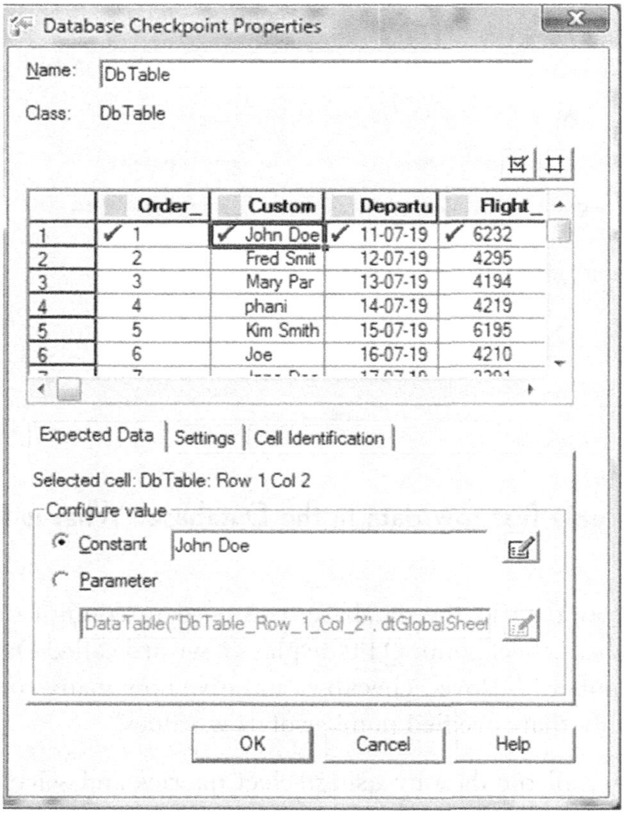

2nd Method

16. How can you check if a particular cell/row/column has a specific type of data?

We can do these types of verifications for Database and Table Checkpoints as the Table and Database will have Rows, Columns and Cells.

To verify the type of data in a particular cell, we have to configure Database and Table Checkpoint settings. The settings are available in respective checkpoint windows. We can do only Numeric and String type of data verification.

To Apply settings, select the cells which you want to verify and select the verification you want to perform.

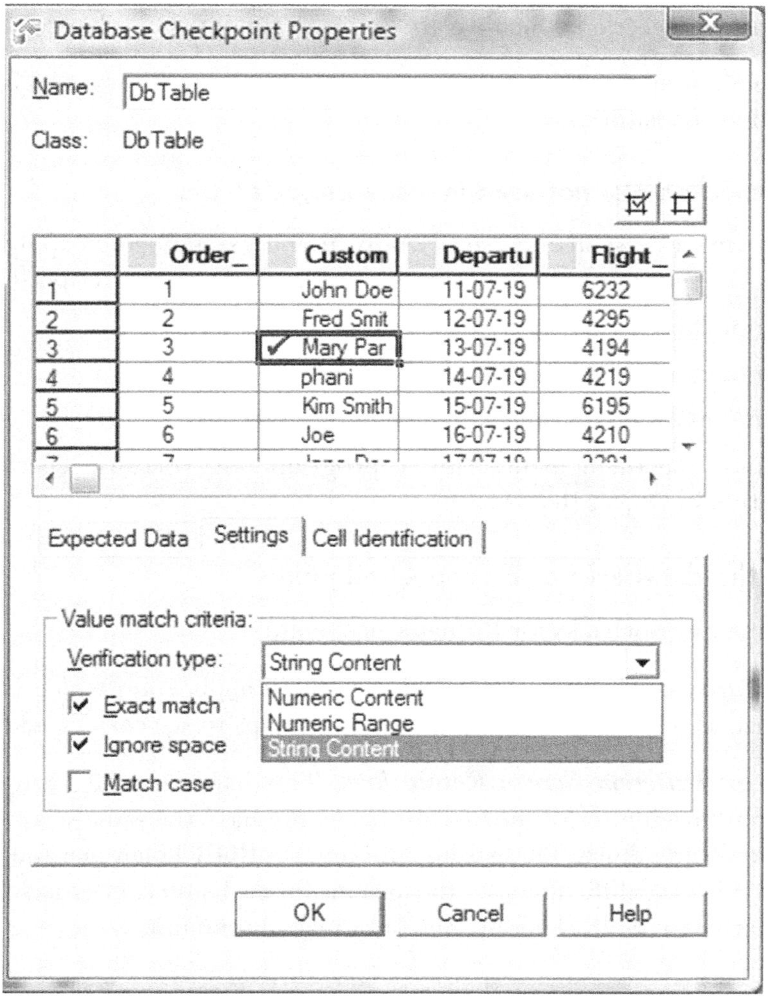

Database Checkpoint data type verification

17. How can you use one script checkpoint in another script?

We know that check point stores its information in Object Repository. To use a check point in other actions, we must copy the checkpoint from source action repository and paste it in destination action repository. We can copy and paste checkpoints between object repositories using Object Repository Manager.

Once the check point is copied, associate that repository to any action and use below statement to apply the check point.

```
Object.Check CheckPoint("CheckPointName")
```

Here Object is a test object on which we are going to apply the check point.

CheckPointName is the checkpoint name exists in object repository which we have copied from source action repository.

18. Why are checkpoints not used in many projects?

Though checkpoints are useful and user friendly in understanding and applying, due to some limitations those are not useful for many projects. The limitations are specified below.

- ➢ We cannot check all the properties whatever we want.
- ➢ We cannot control them by using scripting
- ➢ We cannot use the same checkpoint for other objects
- ➢ We cannot use them in descriptive programming (Because checkpoint stores its information in Object Repository)

19. What are the drawbacks of Bitmap Checkpoints?

There are two major drawbacks for Bitmap Checkpoints

No Facility to Parameterize: We are working with an application which is having country maps. In this case we require parameterization of bitmaps to see correct map is displayed.

May not work on Different Screen Resolutions: This happens when you want to run the scripts on different machines. All the machines may not have the same screen resolution. Due to this it leads to script failure. There is an option to set RGB Tolerance and Pixel for Bitmap checkpoint. But it is very difficult to set the options for each and every machine, as there is no scripting alternative to modify the settings of bitmap checkpoint.

20. How do you apply Page/Table/Image Checkpoint?

By default, QTP doesn't display Page, Image and Table Checkpoints in checkpoints list. If you apply the Standard CheckPoint on Web Page object, that will convert to Page Checkpoint.

If you apply Image CheckPoint on Web Image object, that will convert to Image Checkpoint.

If you apply Table CheckPoint on any add-in environment Table or List view objects, that will convert to Table Checkpoint.

21. What type of verifications can be performed using Page Checkpoint?

We can check the following:

Page Properties

- ➢ Load Time
- ➢ Number of Images
- ➢ Number of Links

HTML Verification

- ➢ HTML Source
- ➢ HTML Tags

Also, we can check the URL's of links, sources of images and the broken links.

22. How can you check property of an object without using a checkpoint?

The below statement is useful to check property of an object. But it checks only one property at a time.

```
Object.CheckProperty "Property Name","Property Value","Timeout"
```

Here Object is a test object.

23. What are the drawbacks of check points?

Refer 18th Question Answer

24. What is the use of Database Checkpoint?

Database checkpoint is to check the data in the database. We can use this in checking the databases accessed by your application. A DB Query is required to retrieve the data from database. The retrieved data will be used as expected value to verify the database in next time for the actual/current result of the same query.

25. I want to check text in a WebTable. Which check point is useful Text or Table Checkpoint? Explain?

For this we can use Text and Table checkpoints. To check the cell by cell text of a web table, we can use Table checkpoint. To check the complete text without considering table cells, we can use Text checkpoint.

26. What is Checkpoint Timeout?

QTP executes a checkpoint and waits for success in verification. If checkpoint fails it waits for the specified timeout and until reaching the timeout, QTP keeps on verifying the success of the checkpoint. Within the timeout, if Checkpoint passes, it returns pass status, QTP will not wait to complete the timeout time.

27. How do you edit an inserted checkpoint?

Checkpoints can be edited in two ways:

From Object Repository: The check point stores its information in Object Repository. To edit the checkpoint, open respective Action Object Repository and select the check point which you want to modify under Checkpoint and Output Objects. In the right side you can see the edited checkpoint properties, and you can modify the checkpoint, based on your requirements.

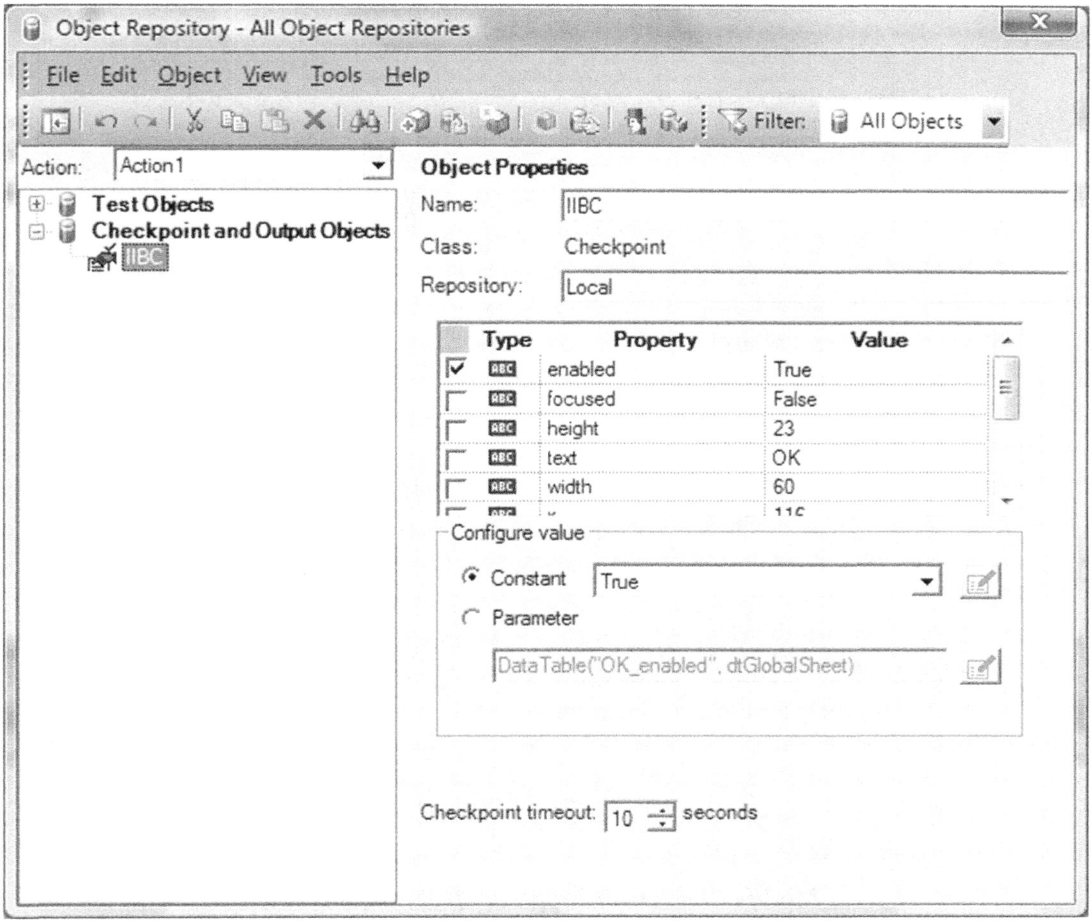

From Script: Go to the statement where the check point is applied, right click on check point name, in the options select "Checkpoint Properties", In the open dialog box do the required modifications.

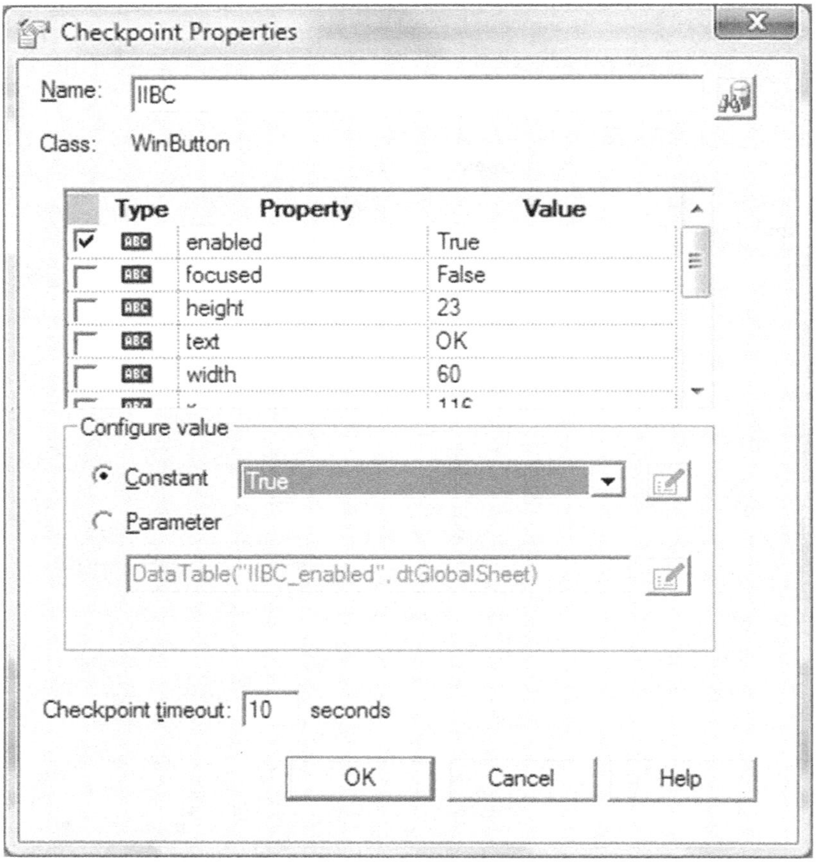

Modify Checkpoint Properties from Expert View

28. Is it possible to create checkpoints in Descriptive Programming? Explain.

Checkpoints cannot be created in Descriptive Programming because checkpoint stores its information in Object Repository.

29. On what type of objects can we apply Table Checkpoint?

Table Checkpoint supports all GUI environments. We can apply these on all table objects which are there in other add-in environments. These are also supported for list view objects, such as WinListView and VbListView, as well as other list view objects in add-in environments.

CHAPTER 7

Parameterization

1. What is a Parameter and Parameterization?

A Parameter is like a variable which can contain a value. The value of the parameter can be assigned by the internal/external data source or generator.

Parameterization is the process of replacing the values with Parameters. When you replace the values with parameters, the test can have the facility of Data driving.

2. What is the difference between Parameterization and Data driving?

Parameterization enables to do data driving for a script. Running a script with different sets of data is called as Data Driving. Once a test is parameterized, we can run it by using different sets of data from external data sources like excel sheets. That is called a data driven test.

3. Explain Types in Parameterization.

There are 4 types of Parameters

Datatable Parameters: QTP has an in built Datatable which is used to store or retrieve values from/to script. Using Datatable parameters are useful to store or retrieve values from Datatable. We can even import external data to data table for later use in the script. This parameterization type is mainly used for Datadriven testing.

Action Parameters: A Reusable Action can be called from another Action. We can send/ retrieve values from/to the Action while calling it. For this Action Parameters are useful.

Action Parameters are of two types.

Input Action Parameters: Useful to send values to an Action while calling it from other Actions.

Output Action Parameters: Useful to retrieve values from an Action while calling it from other Actions.

Environment Parameters: Environment Parameters give environment information of QTP like what is the current OS, Current Test Name and current logged in user...etc.

Environment Parameters are useful to set the global values for a project/test. There are two types in Environment Parameters.

Built-in Environment Parameters: These are defined by QTP, and will have environment details of QTP.

User Defined Environment Parameters: These should be defined by a user, as a standard user will define Application related environment like current execution environment, URL of the application...etc.

User defined environment variables can be stored in outside of QTP. Those are called as external user defined environment variables.

RandomNumber Parameters: These are useful to generate random numbers between a specific range. The Random numbers can be generated for each Action or Test Iteration.

4. What Parameterization Types are useful for Data driven testing?

Datatable Parameterization is useful to data driven testing. Because we can send multiple rows of data from excel sheets by importing them in QTP.

5. How do you Parameterize the Data with External Data Sheet?

By importing that sheet to QTP, we can parameterize External Data Sheet.

6. How do you prepare Data Driven Tests?

After developing the script I will parameterize the data with Datatable Parameters. I will import the data from an external data sheet and use that data in script. By this we can execute the test with multiple rows of test data.

7. How can you Export/Import Environment Variables?

Environment variables can be imported/exported from Test settings dialog.

Go to *File→Settings→Environment→Variable Type: User Defined.* Here we can define environment variables by clicking on Add (+) button. After Adding Environment variables, we can export them by clicking on export button.

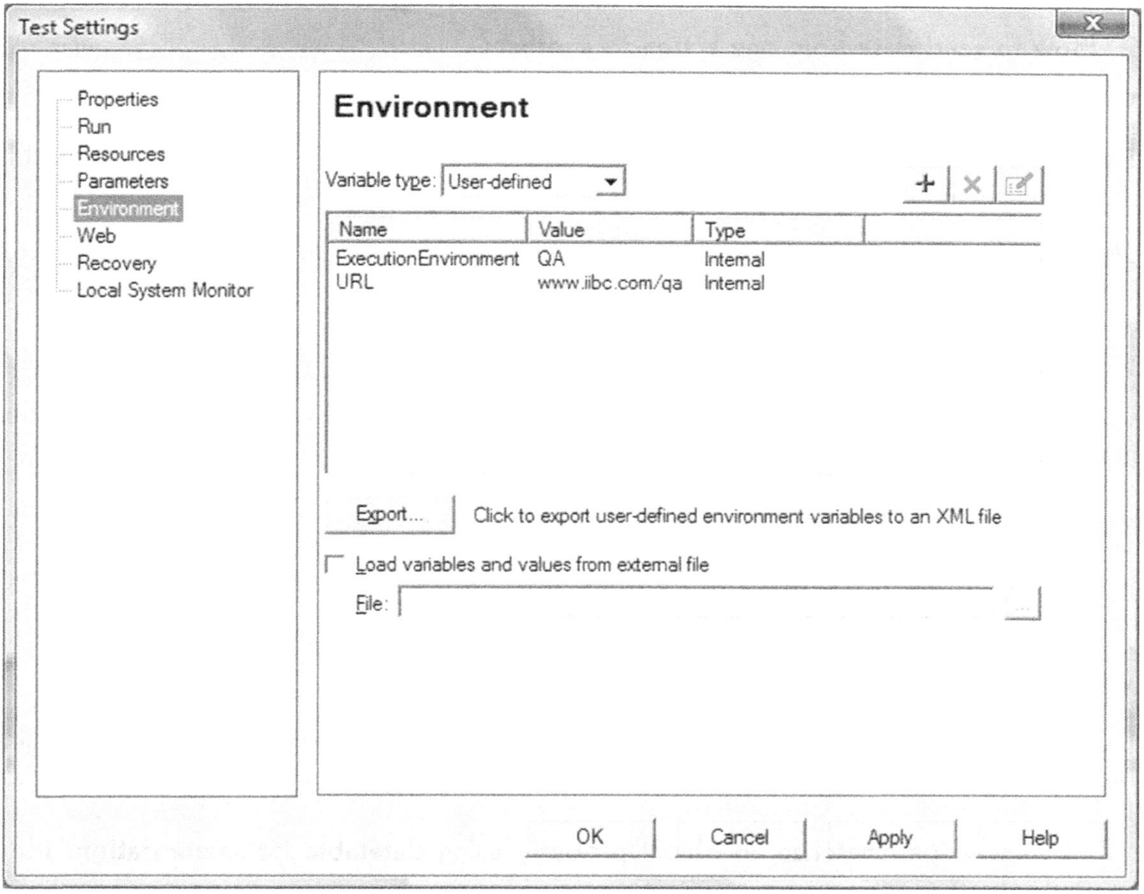

Using load variables and values from external file option, we can specify external environment variable.

8. What type of data can be sent from one action to another?

We can send only below data types from one action to another.

- ➢ String
- ➢ Boolean

- Date
- Number
- Password

9. How to send data from one action to another?

We can use multiple techniques for this.

Using Action Parameters: We can send values between actions but in order to perform this, the action should be called from another action.

Using Environment Parameters: The environment variables are global and we can create the environment variables and store the values in runtime. So we can directly access the values from one action to another without calling it.

Using Datatable Parameters: The data table parameters are useful to store and retrieve values. We can store the values of one action and retrieve the same values from another action in runtime without calling an action from another.

10. What type of data can be sent between Actions?

Using Action/datatable parameters we can send only fixed values. But using the environment parameters we can send any type of data between Actions.

11. What type of data can be parameterized?

Using the Traditional Parameterization defined by QTP we can parameterize only the data. But by using scripting we can do parameterization of any type of data.

12. I want to parameterize an object property using datatable Parameterization. How can I do that?

There is a facility to parameterize object properties in Object Repository. In Object Repository, if you edit any property value by clicking on configure button, a value configuration dialog will be opened.

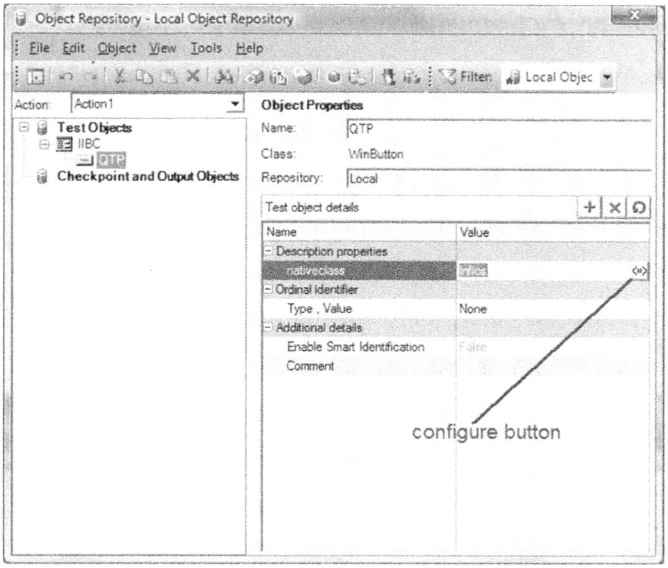

Value configuration dialog has an option called parameter which enables parameterization. Here we can select the type of parameterization and configure the parameters.

13. How do you call an Action with input and output parameters?

Runaction "ActionName",Iterations,InputParameters,OutputParameters

Here, all the input parameters of the action should be specified. If you don't want to send any value, leave it as empty without giving any data but make sure that you give comma.

For example an action has 2 input and 1 output parameters defined, calling that action should be like below.

Runaction "ActionName", Iterations,"ipvalue1","ipvalue2","opvalue1"

In this you don't want to send the 1st input value, leave it as blank but comma should be there.

Runaction "ActionName", Iterations,,"ipvalue2","opvalue1"

14. How do you Parameterize Object Names in Script?

Instead of object name we have to use parameters.

Ex:

Browser("IIBC").Page("IIBC").WebButton("Submit").Click

From the above statement I want to parameterize the name **submit** with another value from repository.

To do this we can write the required logical names in datatable and use datatable parameters instead of submit.

Browser("IIBC").Page("IIBC").WebButton(Datatable("ParameterName","SheetName").Click

15. I have a datatable which is available in Local Drive. How can I import that data to my Action Sheet, without using Scripting Techniques?

We can import the data to QTP datatable by selecting an option from datatable.

Right click on QTP Datable→Sheet→ImportFrom File and Select the excel sheet.

Automatically the data in the excel sheet will get imported.

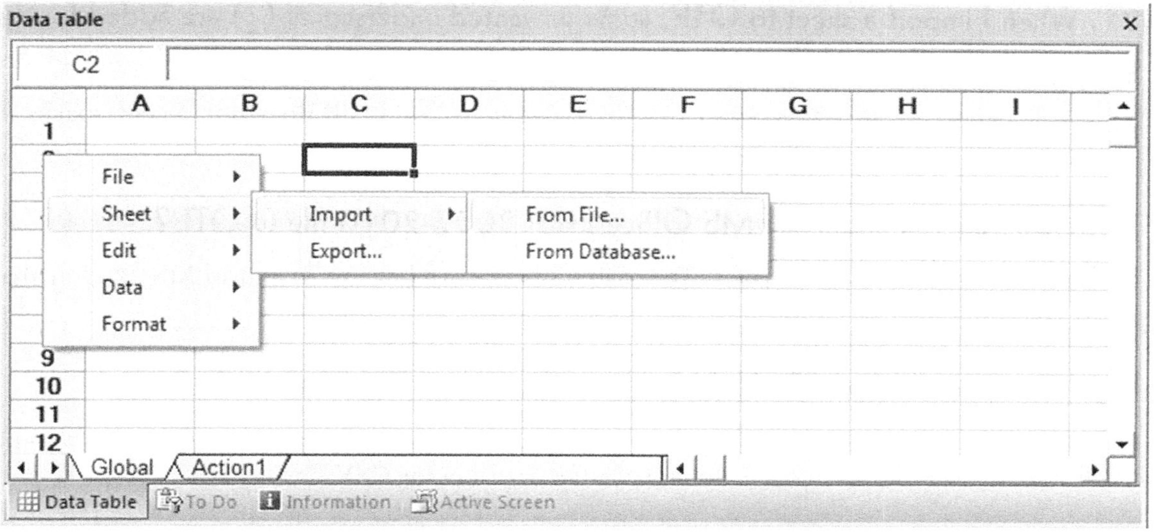

16. What is the statement to Parameterize data using Datatable Parameters?

Datatable("ColumnName","SheetName")

17. What is the statement to Parameterize data using Environment Parameters?

Environment("ParameterName") or Environment.Value("ParameterName")

18. What type of files can be used to store User Defined Environment Variables?

XML files and INI files are used. But now QTP does not support **ini** files. Upto QTP 9.2 we can use ini files.

19. How do you find if a variable is added from External Environment File?

The external variable will be coloured in blue. Using that, we can identify it as external variable.

20. What is the difference between QTP Datatable and Excel Sheet?

The first row values in Excel Sheet will become the column names in QTP datasheet. We can use data however we want in excel sheets and we can assign column names wherever we want. But QTP datatable column names should not have a space. The complex formulas will not work in QTP datatable.

21. When I import a sheet to QTP, some unwanted underscores (_) are added for the columns names of that sheet. Why does this problem occurr?

This will happen if you have spaces in the column names. QTP does not accept spaces in column names. So it will automatically replace spaces with underscores.

22. How can you import an MS Office Excel 2007-2010 file to QTP?

We cannot import xlsx file format. To work with that we have to save it in MS 2003 format with xls.

23. I have the data in a csv file. How can I implement Parameterization?

CSV File cannot import to the datatable like how a datatable can import to QTP. We should use scripting techniques in order to do parameterization for CSV files.

24. My application data is available in a Database. How can I implement Parameterization?

You can import data to QTP datatable from DB by using import option provided by QTP datatable. Observe below screen.

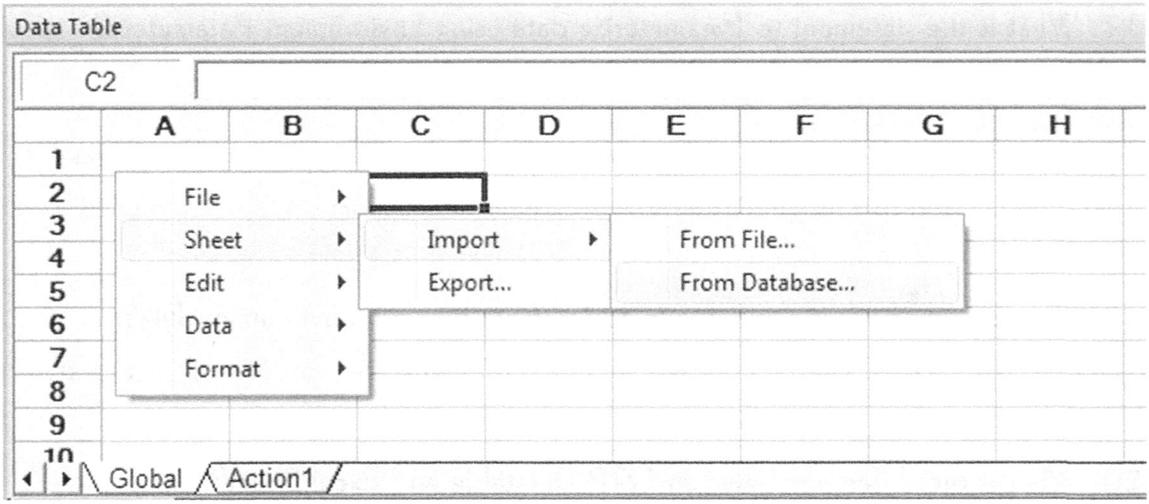

If you select "from Database", Database Query Wizard dialog will open. Using SQL query you can import data from database and use datatable parameters to do parameterization.

25. What is Runtime Data? Where is it stored?

Run time data is the data created or used in runtime. We can store and retrieve the values from datatable. Before completing the execution whatever the data we have in datatables, the data will be sent to result page. That is nothing but runtime data and the datatable is called as runtime Datatable. And it will be in Readable mode.

CHAPTER 8

Synchronization

1. What is Synchronization?

When you run a script, the application may not respond with the same speed of script. Synchronization is the process of adjusting the time gap between Script speed and Application speed.

2. How Synchronization Concept was implemented in your Project?

We have used all the synchronization techniques in our project.

Synchronization Point: We have used wait property for some of the situations where we have waited for the property values.

Wait: We have used wait statement in some of the situations where we are not waiting for any object property/object. But we are waiting for data.

Exist: We have used it for checking object existence.

Object Synchronization Timeout: QTP automatically uses this. QTP waits for an object to load before running a step in the test.

Sync: We have used it for Browser and Page synchronization.

3. An object is not identified by QTP. How much time does QTP wait?

This is dependent on how many seconds are specified in Object Synchronization Timeout at File→ Settings→Run→Object Synchronization Timeout

By default QTP waits for 20 seconds.

4. Window("IIBC").Winbutton("Infics").Exist(10) In this statement the button "Infics" is not identified. How much time does QTP wait?

This waits for 10 seconds. When QTP is checking for an object using "exist" property, it will not consider object synchronization timeout.

5. What is the difference between wait and wait property?

Wait is mandatory and Waitproperty is optional.

When wait(10) is used, the test should wait for 10 seconds where as 10 seconds is optional for waitproperty because this statement waits for a property value to be matched. Whenever the property value matches with in the specified timeout, the test will not wait for complete time.

6. When to use Wait Property?

Wait property is useful when there is a need to wait for a property value of an object.

Ex: A status message to appear on an object, for a button to become enabled

7. When to use Wait?

Wait statement is useful in some of the situations where we are not waiting for any object property/object. But we are waiting for data.

Ex: After selecting a country in country list box, we might need to wait for some fixed time to load the states in states list box.

8. When to use Exist?

Exist is useful when we want to wait for a window/dialog/object existence.

9. What is ReadyState native property of a browser?

ReadyState is a native property for browser to tell the status of the browser navigation. This property contains any of the value from 0 to 4. Each value has a different meaning.

ReadyState= 0 (Just initialized)

ReadyState= 1 (Object currently loading its properties)

ReadyState= 2 (Object was initialized)

ReadyState= 3 (Object is interactive, but not all its data is available)

ReadyState= 4 (Object has received all its data)

Some of the projects are using ReadyState property for synchronizing purpose.

10. What is Object Synchronization Time Out?

QTP automatically uses this. QTP waits for an object to load before running a step in the test. This can be configured at File→Settings→Run→Object Synchronization Timeout

11. What is the maximum timeout for Object Synchronization Time Out?

1000 seconds

12. What is Browser Navigation Timeout?

QTP automatically uses this. QTP waits for a webpage to load before running a step in the test. This can be configured at File→Settings→ Web→Browser Navigation Timeout

13. What is the difference between Exist and WaitProperty?

These two are optional waits and the way how we use these two are different. The exist is applied to see the object existence, where as WaitProperty is to wait for a property of an existing object.

14. I clicked on a link. What synchronization technique is to be used to wait for loading the page?

Sync is useful in such situations because the page will get navigated when clicked on a link.

15. In the Results page, the Synchronization Point Result shows a warning. What does it mean?

This means that the synchronization point has reached the timeout and the property value has not matched.

CHAPTER 9

Recovery Scenarios

1. What is an Exception? How did you handle Exceptions in your project?

An exception is an unexpected or unwanted event or error because of which application crashes leading to test failure.

We have used recovery scenarios to handle the exceptions. We have called functions within the recovery scenarios to handle these exceptions.

2. What is the process of creating a Recovery Scenario?

Below is the process of creating recovery scenario

- defining the trigger event that interrupts the run session
- specifying the recovery operations required to continue
- choosing a post-recovery test run operation
- specifying a name and description for the recovery scenario
- (for tests) specifying whether to associate the recovery scenario to the current test and/or to all new tests

3. How exactly does the Recovery Scenario Mechanism Works?

When QTP gets an error, it will check for any associated recovery scenarios. If any recovery is associated, QTP will identify the object/condition specified in trigger event. If that object/

condition matches, then QTP executes the specified Recovery Operation. Specified Post Recovery Operation will also be executed after executing the Recovery Operation.

4. What are the different reasons which will generate errors in your project?

If we get an error, that is because of 3 reasons

Script Issue: A poor script development will give poor result. Because of this we get Test Run Errors.

Application Issue: Application generates unwanted pop ups or throughs unexpected events in script runtime.

Environment Issue: Application suddenly crashes because of environment issue.

5. How is Recovery Scenario Manager useful in handling Exceptions?

Recovery Scenario Manager enables you to create Recovery Scenarios to handle the exceptions generated by Script, Application and Environment. We can specify Recovery Operations within a Recovery Scenario to handle the exceptions. Those Recovery Operations will be executed whenever an exception has occurred in Test Runtime.

6. How do you handle the exceptions generated by application?

There are two types of Exceptions that will be generated by Application

Unwanted Popup windows: The unwanted/unexpected Popup windows will disrupt the Script and cause the failure. To handle them we have used Popup Recovery Scenario. In this, we have specified the window name and how to handle it by using a recovery operation.

Object Related Errors: Sometimes we get errors like "Page cannot be displayed" or an application is opened, due to an internal problem, the window is not responding and all of the objects are in disable state. In this case, we can use Object State Recovery Scenario which will execute a Recovery Operation based on Object State that is already provided by you when creating it.

7. How do you handle the exceptions generated by QTP?

QTP generates exceptions and those are called as Test Run Errors. We can handle only Object and Object Data Related Test Run Errors. The errors are

- Item in Menu or List Not unique
- Item in Menu or List not found

- More than One Object Respond to its physical description
- Object is disabled
- Object not found
- Object not visible

These errors can be handled by Test Run Error Recovery Scenario. In this we can specify the error and what operation is required to perform based on the error.

8. How do you handle the exceptions raised because of environment?

An environment issue causes the Application Crash or No Response from the Application. For Application Crashes we use the Application Crash Recovery Scenario. We can define a recovery scenario to set the application normal. For No Response we can use Object State Recovery Scenario to perform a Recovery Operation.

9. What is trigger event?

Trigger Event is an event that interrupts your run session which will cause Test Failure. This can happen in both QTP and application.

10. What is Recovery Operation?

The operation which recovers QTP to run the test after a trigger event interrupts the run session.

11. What are the types in Recovery Operations?

Function Call: We can specify a function to be executed when performing the recovery operation.

Keyboard or Mouse Operation: In this, there are multiple sub operations

- Click Default button / Press the ENTER key
- Click Cancel button / Press the ESCAPE key
- Click button with label
- Press key or key combination

By using Click button with label, we can specify a button which is there in the application. By using Press key or Key combination, we can specify a key to be pressed or with a combination ctrl/alt to be pressed in the recovery operation.

Close Application Process: We can specify a process to be closed when you get an error. It will display current running list of processes in your machine. We can choose any of the process to be closed when that Recovery Scenario is executed.

12. Where do you write Recovery Functions?

We can write Recovery Functions in Libraries and specify those libraries when creating the recovery scenario. We can create libraries from QTP using Create new function library option. We can also use vbs or txt files as libraries.

13. How many recovery scenarios have been developed in your project?

We have developed over 10 recovery scenarios for below purposes

- ➢ To handle a message that is displayed when an ActiveX object on an Internet Explorer page may be unsafe.
- ➢ To handle Internet Explorer ASP errors
- ➢ To handle a message that is displayed when a file is selected for download.
- ➢ To handle a message that is displayed when Internet Explorer is about to redirect to a new Internet site.
- ➢ To handle a message that is displayed when an object cannot be found in Internet Explorer.
- ➢ To handle security Alerts
- ➢ To handle Application Generated Object Related Exceptions
- ➢ To handle QTP Generated Exceptions
- ➢ To handle Application Crashes

14. What are the recovery scenarios used in your project?

We have used all of the recovery scenarios Popup, ObjectState, TestRunError and Application Crash.

15. What is the extension for Recovery Scenario File?

QRS – Quicktest Recovery Scenario

16. How did you maintain the recovery scenarios?

We can create all Recovery Scenarios in one Recovery file. Because of that, very less maintenance is required. In prepared Recovery Scenarios if any window title is changed or process name is changed or object state is changed, we have to keep an update to ensure that the specified Window/ObjectState/Processes for Trigger events are correct.

17. Can I use recovery scenarios developed for one project in other projects?

Yes. All Recovery Scenarios are shared. We can have generic scenarios to handle Browser Security Alerts, Download messages or any error related to the browser not to the loaded html document. These scenarios can be used for other projects.

18. When do you prepare the Recovery Scenarios?

Recovery Scenarios can be prepared any time of Development or Execution of the Test because the events are unpredictable. Some can be identified in the Script Development phase and some can be identified during the test execution time. Whenever an event is identified we can directly develop recovery scenarios.

19. When do you use Recovery Scenarios?

Recovery Scenarios are advised to be used only with events that you cannot predict in advance.

If the error is predictable, it is recommended that you can use '**if**' condition to perform the operation by using any function.

20. What is the difference in direct usage of a function and keeping the function in recovery scenario?

If the error is expected, we can use 'if' condition and specify the function to be executed. Only for that particular situation and for only once it gets executed.

If the error is unexpected we will specify the function in recovery scenario. Because of this, in entire script run whenever and where ever that error occurs, the function will get executed as a recovery operation.

21. What is Post Recovery Operation? When is it useful?

Post Recovery Operation is used to instruct QTP, how to proceed after performing the recovery operation. Sometimes we may require to execute the same failed step again or to skip the entire iteration and to execute next iteration.

22. What is the difference between using "On Error Resume Next" and Recovery Scenarios?

On Error Resume Next will suppress the errors that are generated by QTP. It does not provide alternatives when a step has failed. The aim of On Error Resume Next is to complete the script execution without considering the Application Response.

Recovery Scenarios will provide a recovery to be executed when you get an error. The aim of Recovery Scenario Manager is to provide recoveries whenever an event arises by QTP, Application or by Environment.

23. How do you handle the exceptions without using recovery scenarios?

There is no alternative available for Recovery Scenarios. In some advanced Test Automation Frameworks, they may use some techniques to fulfill the need of Recovery Scenarios but those are limited. They cannot handle all types of unexpected events.

24. Explain Popup Trigger Event.

Popup trigger event is to handle the unexpected/unwanted popup windows which are generated by an Application. In this we can specify a window which interrupts the Test Execution. We can also specify a recovery operation to handle the Popup windows.

25. Explain Object State Trigger Event.

We can specify a specific object state with properties of the object. QTP executes a specified recovery scenario whenever it gets an error and if and only if that object is at specific state.

We can specify a recovery operation to be executed whenever QTP gets an error and at the same time the specified object is at same state.

26. Explain TestRunError Trigger Event?

TestRunError trigger event is used to handle the object related errors that are generated by QTP. QuickTest detects a run error and identifies it by a failed return value from a method. We can specify a recovery operation based on the type of error generated.

27. Explain Application Crash Trigger Event?

An application crash can happen because of an internal problem of the application. QTP detects an application crash and identifies it according to a predefined list of applications. We can specify a recovery operation which to be performed when an application crash is indentified by QTP.

28. How can you use created Recovery Function Parameters for Popup Trigger Event?

When you select function call as the recovery operation for Popup trigger event, the Recovery Scenario Manager gives you the below syntax to develop the function.

The function syntax is like below

```
Function RecoveryFunction1(object)

End Function
```

In this the parameter object is the popup window. When the Recovery Scenario Activates and executes the recovery operation, the parameter object will have the Popupwindow object. To perform any operations on the opened popup window, we can directly use this object parameter.

For example to click on OK button which is displayed in this popup window you can use the recovery function like below.

```
Function RecoveryFunction1(object)

      Object.WinButton("text:=OK").click

End Function
```

For this we don't need to learn any object.

29. How can you use created Recovery Function Parameters for Object State Trigger Event?

When you select function call as the recovery operation for Object State trigger Event, the Recovery Scenario Manager gives you the syntax to develop the function.

The function syntax is like below

```
Function RecoveryFunction1(object)

End Function
```

In this the parameter object is the object which you have selected. When the Recovery Scenario Activates and executes the recovery operation, the parameter object will have the identified object with state. We can directly use this object parameter to find whether the object is disabled or enabled.

For example to wait for object enable we can use below function

```
Function RecoveryFunction1(object)
      If Object.GetROproperty("enabled") = False then
            Object.Waitproperty "enabled",true,10000
      End If
End Function
```

30. How can you use created Recovery Function Parameters for TestRunError Trigger Event?

When you select function call as the recovery operation for TestRunError trigger event, the Recovery Scenario Manager gives you the below syntax to develop the function.

```
Function RecoveryFunction1(Object, Method, Arguments, retVal)
End Function
```

In Test Run Error we will select the error type. The selected error code will be returned to function. For example if we select object in Menu or list is not unique. Then the parameters information is like below

Object: The list object

Method: The methods which you have used to perform operation

Arguments: The list item name

retVal: The error code

The below function will select the list item based on index

```
Function RecoveryFunction1(Object, Method, Arguments, retVal)
      lstItemCount=Object.GetROproperty("items count")
      For iCounter=1 to lstItemCount
            If Object.getitem(iCounter) = Arguments(0) then
                  Object.Method Arguments(0)
                  Exit For
            End If
```

```
      Next
End Function
```

31. How can you use created Recovery Function Parameters for Application Crash Trigger Event?

When you select function call as the recovery operation for Application Crash trigger Event, the Recovery Scenario Manager gives you the syntax to develop the function.

```
Function RecoveryFunction1(ProcessName, ProcessID)
End Function
```

While creating application crash recovery scenario we will select a process name. That process name and process id will become inputs for recovery function.

The below function is to rerun crashed process

```
Function RecoveryFunction1(ProcessName, ProcessID)
      Systemutil.run ProcessName
End Function
```

32. How many scenarios can be created in one Recovery Scenario file?

There is no maximum limit given by HP. We can create as many as we want.

33. How do you Associate Recovery Scenarios for all QTP Tests?

When developing the test we can add a recovery scenario in default settings, automatically that will get added in all sub sequence created tests.

If the tests are already created and you want to associate a recovery scenario then we have to open each test and associate recovery manually. Automation Object Model Concept is useful to add a recovery automatically to a script or to multiple scripts.

The below script will add a recovery scenario to the script.

```
' Create the Application object
Set qtApp = CreateObject("QuickTest.Application")
```

' Return the Recovery object for the current test

```
Set qtTestRecovery = qtApp.Test.Settings.Recovery

' Add the "ErrMessage" scenario as the first scenario
qtTestRecovery.Add "C:\Recovery.qrs", "ErrMessage", 1
```

34. Is it possible to automate the creation of recovery scenarios?

We don't have this facility in QTP like we have in Winrunner automation tool.

35. How to disable Recovery Scenario for a particular Test?

If you don't want to execute a particular scenario then you have to go to

File→Settings→Recovery Deselect the check box beside the recovery scenario

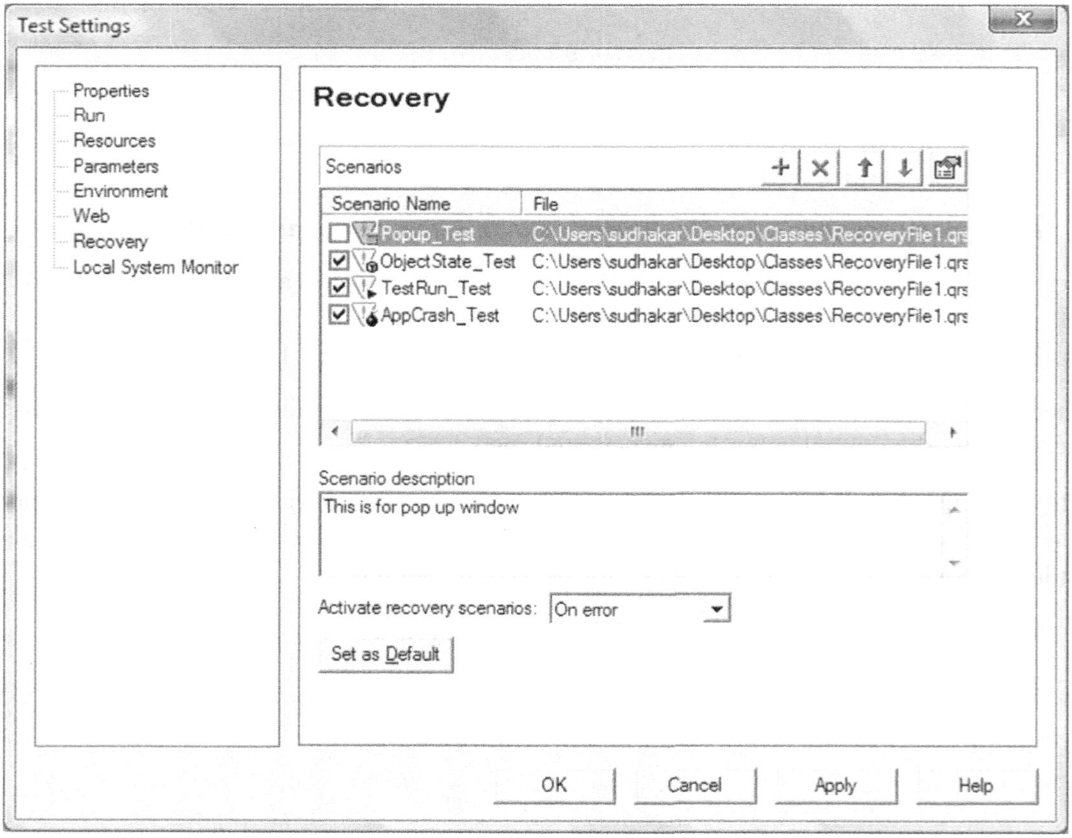

36. Are Recovery Scenarios shared?

Yes. All Recovery Scenarios are shared. We can use for any tests.

37. When a Recovery will get activated?

By default Recovery Scenarios will get activated on errors. Whenever an error is identified by QTP, it looks for any Associated Recovery Scenario. If any Recovery Scenario is associated that will get activated.

38. My Application is generating unwanted popup messages which requires the user to click on OK. But those messages are not Popup windows generated by the browser and when you get this error, the HTML document also will be in active state. How do you handle this situation?

Some applications will have inbuilt html popups. Those are not popup windows but will not allow us to perform any operations. In this case we have to go for object state recovery scenario. In that we can mention the html popup as object and provide a recovery operation to perform. Automatically whenever QTP gets an error and if that html popup exists, the recovery operation will get executed.

39. Sometimes my application will get down and we are unable to access anything. At that time it shows an error or "Page cannot be displayed" page. How do you handle this situation?

In this situation we have to use object state recovery scenario. Specify *cannot identify page* object, in properties add the page title property and specify recovery operation.

40. Why is there a wait time before Recovery Scenario Executes?

Recovery Scenario will be activated only when QTP identifies an error. So when QTP identifies an error related to object identification, QTP waits for successfulness. In this process the object synchronization timeout will be used to wait. How many seconds are specified in that, that much time QTP will wait.

41. Can Recovery Scenario Handle Syntax Errors?

No.

42. Can Recovery Scenario Handle Array size Type mismatch Errors?

No.

43. What type of errors can be handled by Recovery Scenarios?

Only the errors related to Test Objects.

44. Can Recovery Scenario Handle VB Script Run Time Errors?

No.

45. I have used wrong method for an object. Can recovery scenario handle this?

No.

46. When to use "Keyboard or mouse" and Function call Recovery Operations?

If there is a single operation to be performed and that too if the operation is click then we can go for Keyboard or mouse operation.

If there are multiple steps to be performed or if we need to work with different operations other than click then we have to use Function Call.

CHAPTER 10

Miscellaneous Tool Options

1. How do you configure the Test Execution Flow?

In two ways we can configure the Test Flow.

- In TestFlow Pane
- In Keyword View

The Test Flow pane is specially designed in QTP to configure the Test Flow. Just select an Action and drag it to where ever you want. Follow the same in Keyword view as well

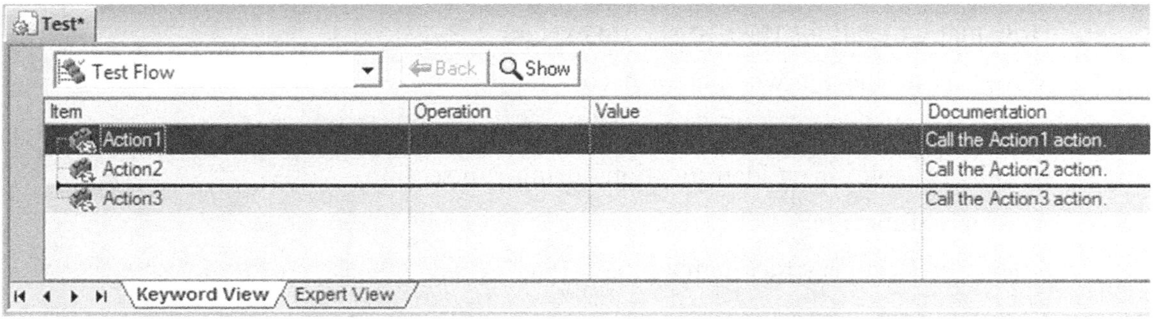

Dragging an Action in keyword view

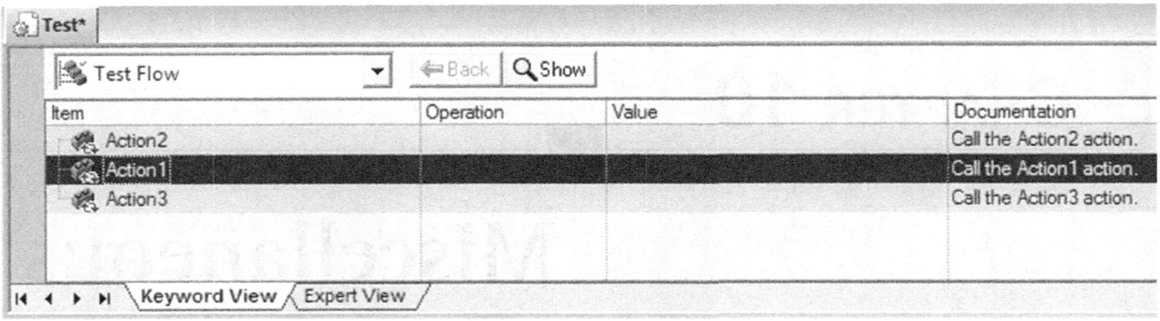

Test Flow is changed

2. What is the drawback if we use Active Screen?

Active Screen stores all images of the application. Because of this the size of the test will become huge. In some cases opening of the test will take a lot of time.

We can configure the Active Screen settings to capture the images only on some specified conditions.

Active Screen Settings can be configured in Tools → Options →Active Screen

3. What is the use of Test Settings and how can you share Test Settings with your Team?

Test Settings are the settings configured by the user for a Test. Some of the settings are listed below.

- How many iterations the test should execute
- What should happen when error occurs
- Object Synchronization Timeout
- Enable/Disable smart identification during run session
- Associate Libraries
- Associate Recovery files ...etc

In a project, everybody will be using the same type of settings. To remove the confusion, one person will set the settings and share it to all other people. To share, there is an option to generate script for the configured settings.

File → Settings → Properties → Click on Generate Script button.

We can save the settings script to a vbs file and pass that vbs file to other team members. By double clicking on that vbs file, the settings will be loaded in the opened Test of QTP.

4. What is the alternative for "On Error Resume Next"?

We can configure what should happen when QTP gets an error in the Test Settings.

To configure it go to File → Settings →Run → Select Proceed to Next Action Iteration

This is the alternative for On Error Resume Next

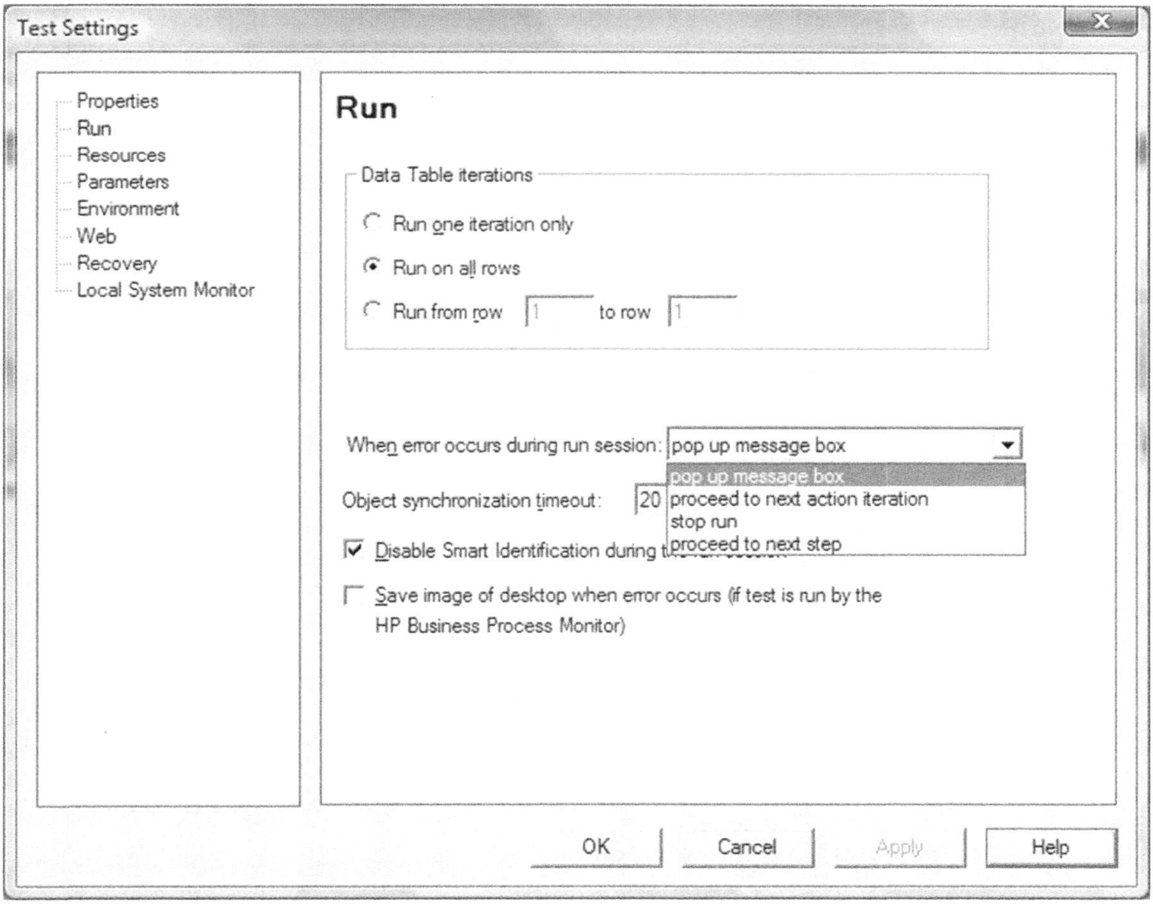

5. How do you associate Function Libraries to a test?

We can associate function libraries in two ways:

In Test Settings: Go to File → Settings → Recourses → Add libraries under Libraries by clicking on Add (+) button.

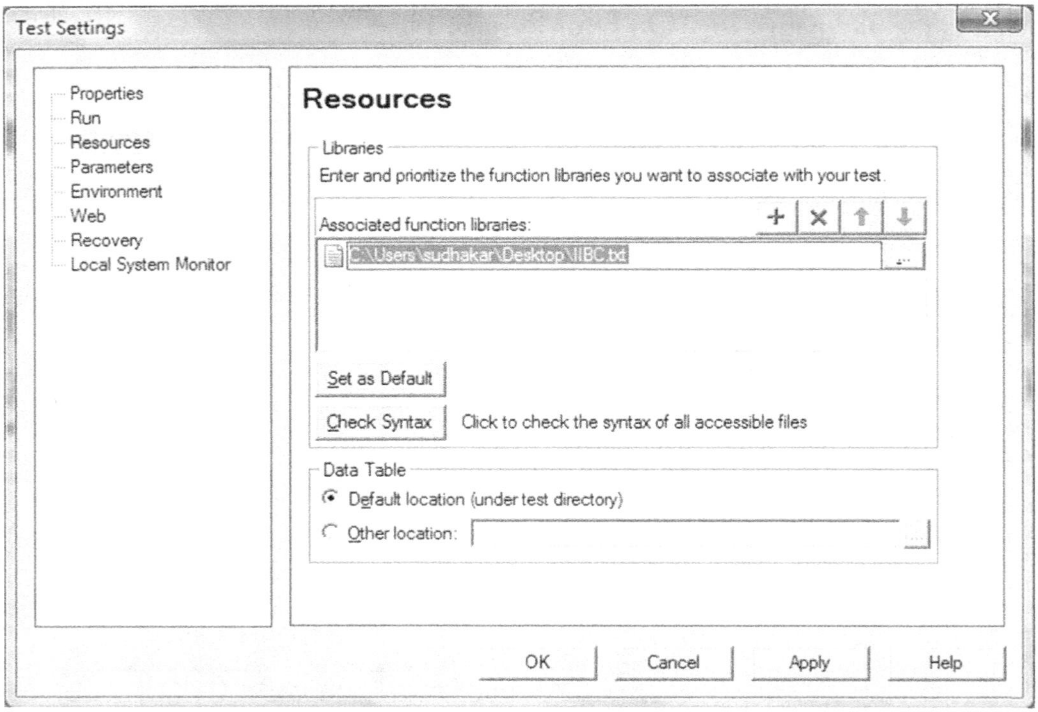

From Resources Pane: In Resources Pane, right click on Associate Function Libraries to Associate a Function Library.

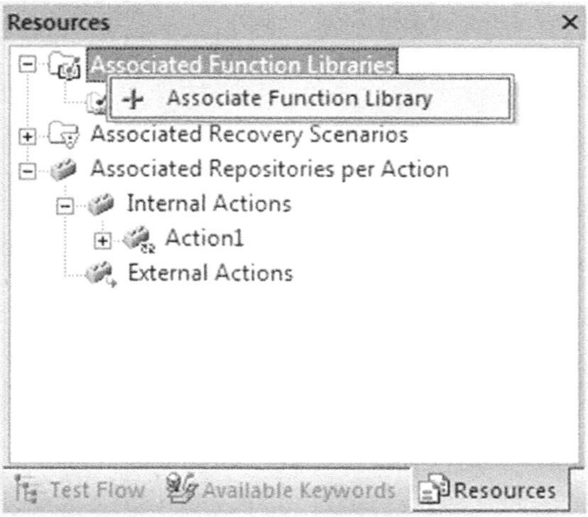

We can also load libraries in runtime by using Executefile Statement, LoadFunctionLibrary Statement (in QTP 11)

6. Is it possible to use external DataTable for QTP? If so how to use?

Yes. We configure it in File → Settings → Resources → Select Other Location under Datatable section. The datatable which you specify should have the Action Names as the sheet names. Otherwise they may fail.

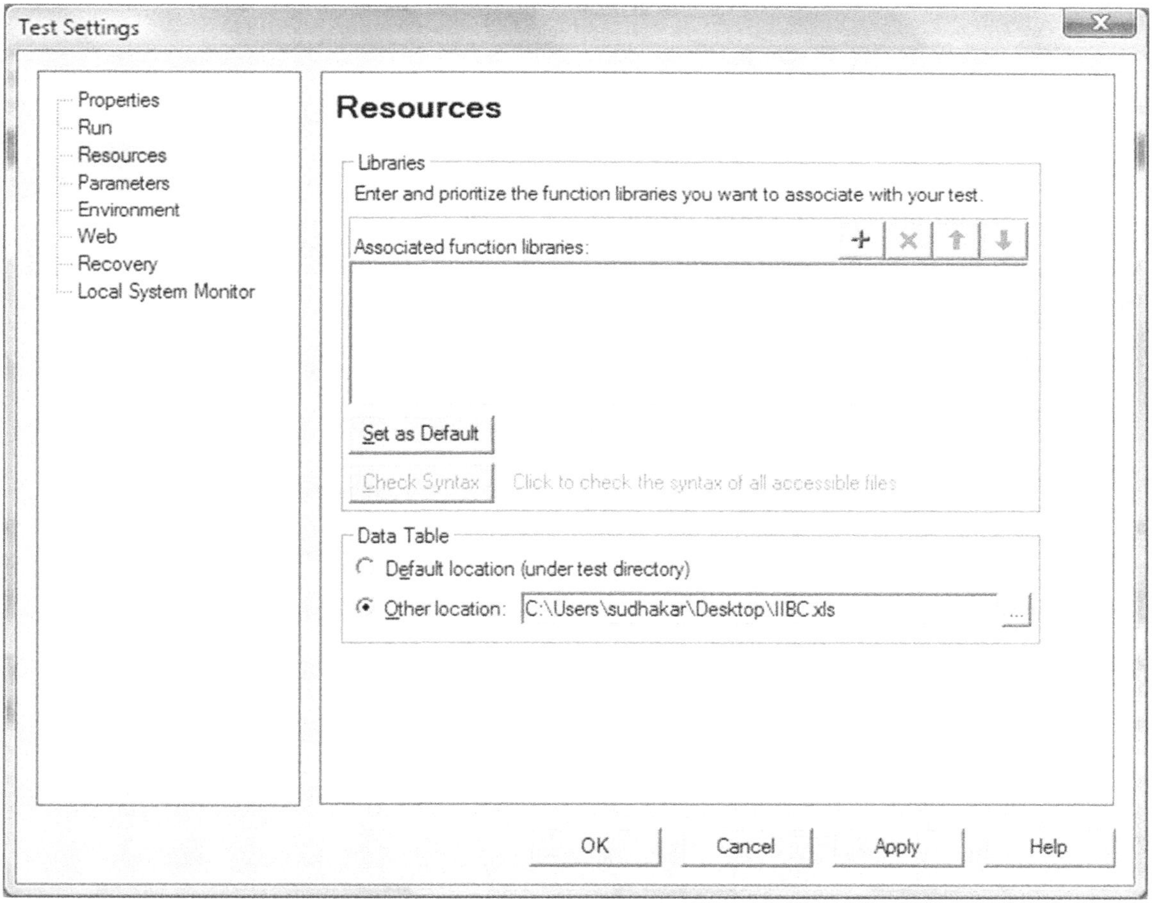

7. How do you connect to QualityCenter?

Go to File → Quality Center Connection → Specify the Server URL, Click on connect

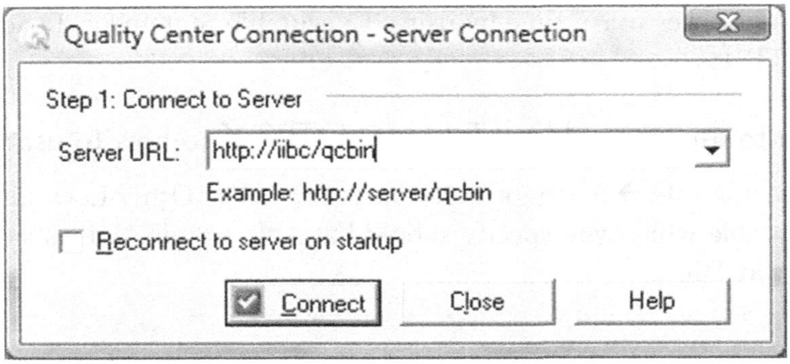

After connecting to the server you will need to specify login credentials and click on Authenticate to access the project.

8. How do you make an Action Reusable?

We can make an Action Reusable in Action Properties Dialog. Go to Edit→Action→Action Properties → Select Reusable Action Checkbox

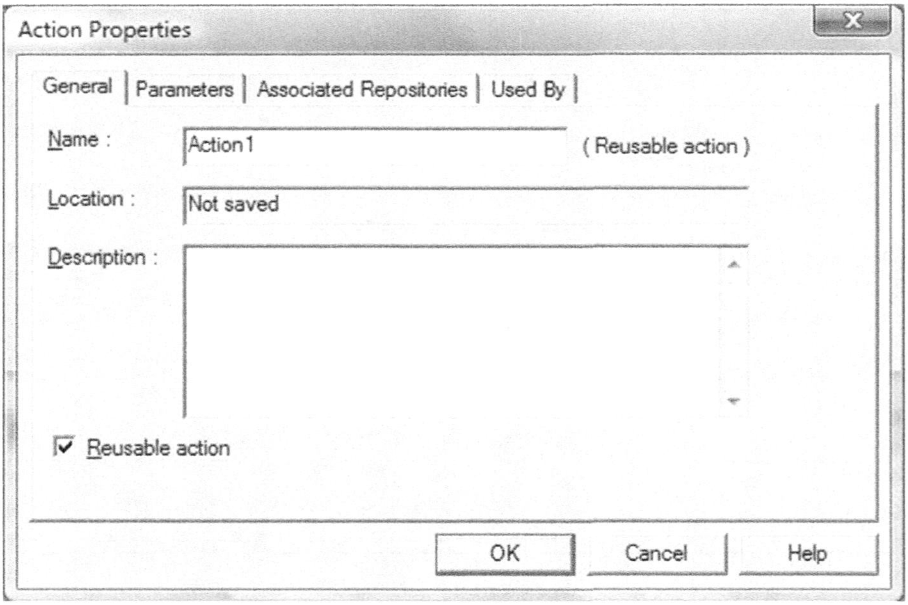

9. What is the use of Action Call Properties dialog?

Action Call Properties are to configure how action should behave when it is called. We can specify how many times the Action should iterate and also specify from where you want to take the value of Action Input Parameter and where you want to store the value of Action Output Parameter.

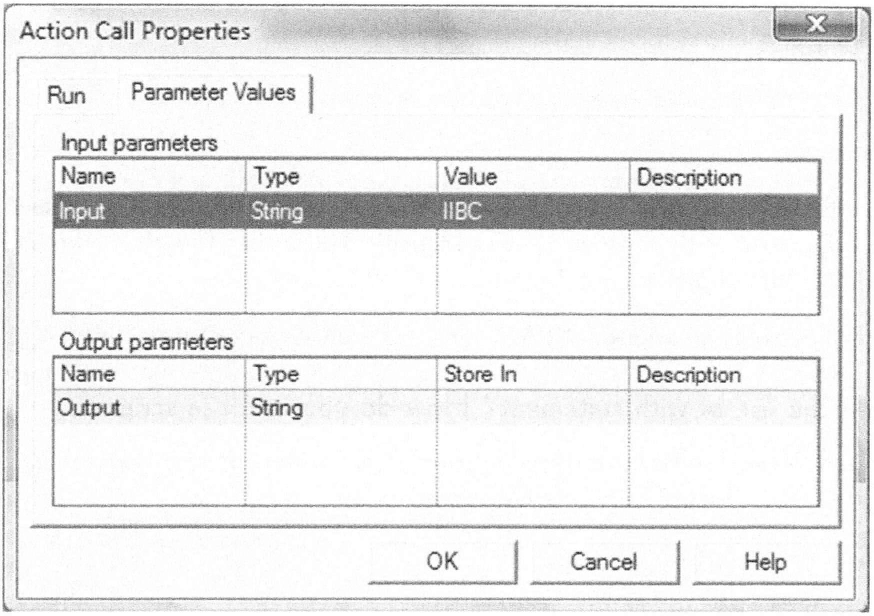

10. What is the difference between Action Properties and Action Call Properties?

Action Properties are to define Action Parameters, Associate Shared Repositories and to make Reusable Action.

Action Call Properties are to configure how action should behave when it is called. The defined Action Parameters can be configured in Action Call Properties dialog.

11. How do you go to particular line in the script?

Use shortcut key CTRL+G

12. How do you comment a statement or block of statements?

Select a statement or bulk of statements and use Shortcut key CTRL+M. We can use rem statement before the step to comment.

13. How do you use Indent and Outdent for script styling?

When developing a script we use conditions, loops or functions. To make readability of the script better, we use indents. Indents are nothing but a tab space character. We can have single and multiple statements and apply indents or outdents.

```
Function Demo()

      Msgbox "This statement started with indent"

End Function
```

In the above function, to make readability of the function better, indent is used for steps in the function. Because of that we can easily identify where that function ends. The same will be applicable for all conditions and loops.

The shortcut key to give indent is "TAB" key, To remove indent use "Shift+Tab" keys.

14. What is the use of with statement? How do you use it in scripts?

With statement is used to remove the repetition of the same object in sequence of statements. It starts with "with Object" and ends with "End With".

For example

```
Browser("IIBC").Page("Infics").WebEdit("UserName").Set "QtpSudhakar"

Browser("IIBC").Page("Infics").WebEdit("Password").Set "QTPIQS"

Browser("IIBC").Page("Infics").WebButton("Register").Click
```

If we apply *with* for the above script, that looks like below

```
With Browser("IIBC").Page("Infics")

      .WebEdit("UserName").Set "QtpSudhakar"

.WebEdit("Password").Set "QTPIQS"

.WebButton("Register").Click

End With
```

15. How do you see the code within a called function which is defined in a library?

In expert view, Right click on the function call and select "Go to Function Definition" to see the code in Function.

Also you can use "Alt+G" to go to where the function is defined.

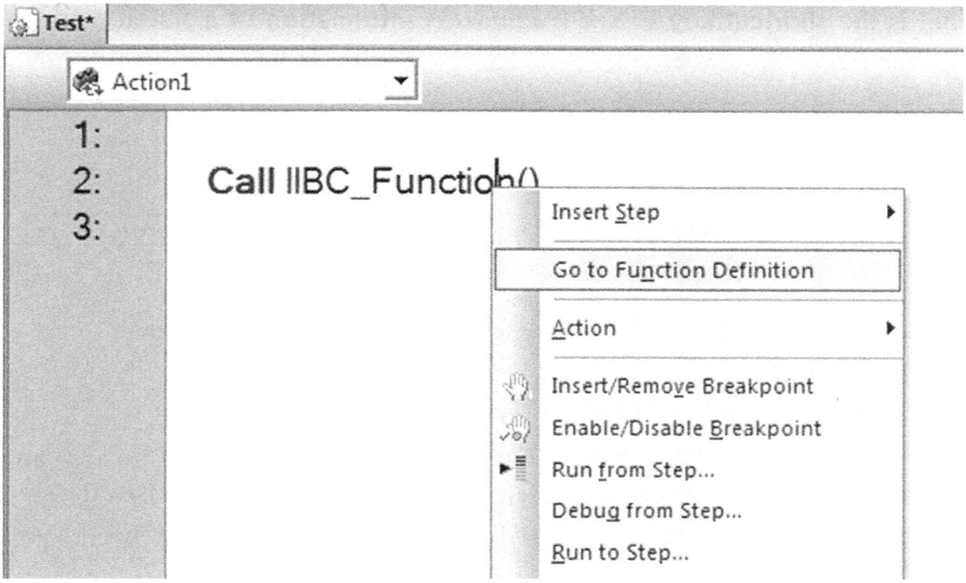

16. How can we see the QTP intelligence/suggestion box?

To see QTP Intelligence use "Ctrl+SpaceBar".

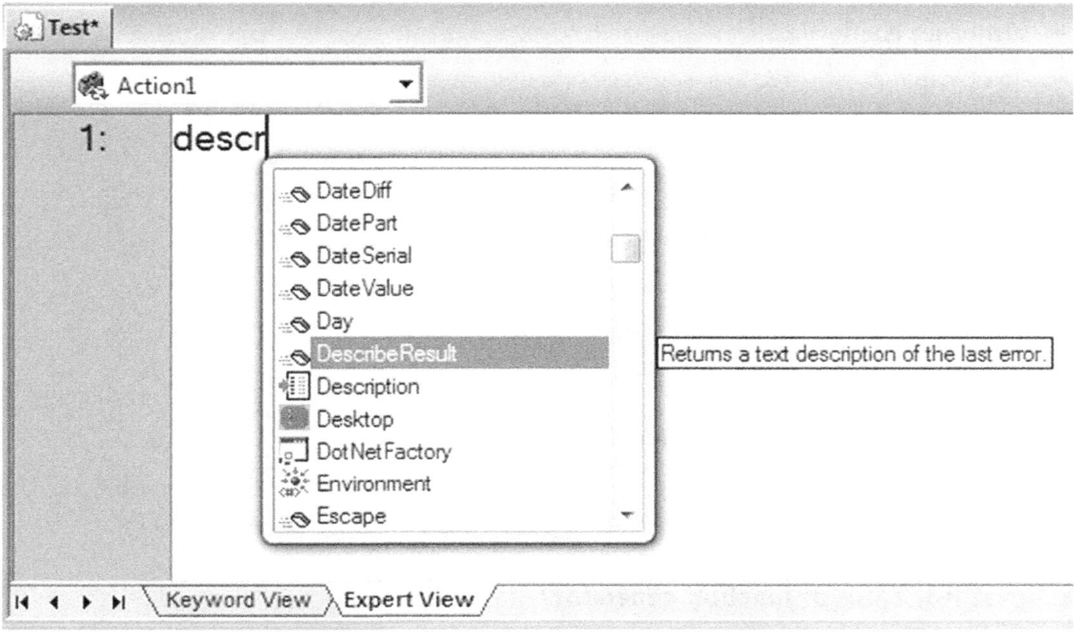

17. What is the shortcut key to see Arguments Information of a statement?

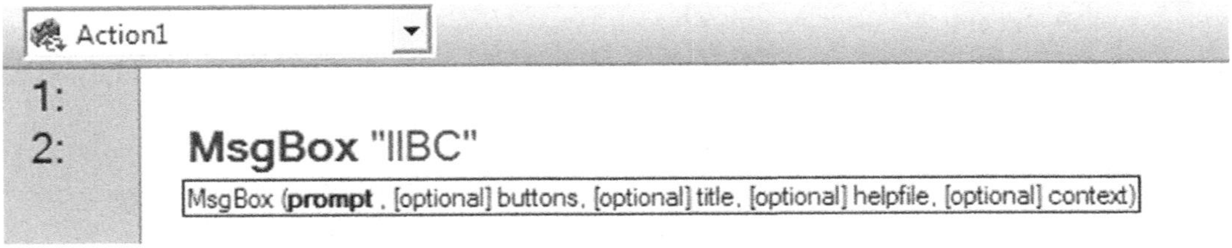

Use "Ctrl + Shift + Spacebar" to see Arguments information of a statement.

18. What is the use of OptionalStep?

OptionalStep is to make a step optional. For example a step has failed because an object is not identified. In this case if you make a step as optional, if the object exists, the step will get executed successfully, if the object is not identified it will not fail. To make a step as optional, use "OptionalStep." in before the step.

By default, QuickTest considers steps that open the following dialog boxes or message boxes as optional steps:

- Auto Complete
- File Download
- Internet Explorer
- Netscape
- Enter Network Password
- Error
- Security Alert
- Security Information
- Security Warning
- Username and Password Required

19. What is the use of Step Generator?

Step Generator is used to generate steps. We can generate steps on Test objects, Utility Objects and function calls. This is useful for the beginners and learners of QTP.

20. What is the use of function generator?

Function Definition Generator is used to generate function definition. We can select type of function, Function name and Type of parameters. Like step generator, this is also useful for beginners and learners to create functions.

21. How do you call Winrunner Test or Function in QTP?

Go to Insert → Call to WinRunner → Test or Function → Browse the WinRunner Test/ Function

To do this WinRunner must be installed in the machine where you execute the script.

22. What is the use of Transactions?

Transactions are used to identify the execution time taken for a step or group of steps. To insert transactions we have to use

Insert→Start Transaction

Insert→ End Transaction

Transactions are more useful to design tests with respect to Performance Testing.

23. Explain Output Values in QTP?

An output value step is a step in which one or more values are captured at a specific point in your test and stored for the duration of the run session. The values can later be used as input at a different point in the run session. We can store output values in Datatables, Environment Parameters and Action Parameters.

The below are the types in output values

- Standard Output Value
- Text Output Value
- TextArea Output Value
- Database Output Value
- XML Output Value (From Application)
- XML Output Value (From Resource)

24. What is the difference between Checkpoints and Output Values?

Checkpoints are for checking purpose. When you insert a checkpoint, it captures expected values from application and checks for the same whenever you run the test.

When you insert an Output Value, it captures value from Application and we can specify a location to store the value. When you run the test, the current value will be stored in the specified location.

25. How do you configure Record and Run settings?

Record and Run settings are used to specify some conditions on how to record and run. We can specify our tests to be executed / recorded on a specific browser or a window. Based on the installed add-in, the record and run settings will be displayed setting for those added add-ins. To configure these settings go to Automation → Record and Run Settings

If you want to execute your scripts only on http://www.i2brightcareers.com by using internet explorer, specify the URL at URL section and select type of browser from the list. You will be able to record and run only on that particular browser and address.

26. What are the different Run Modes in QTP?

The below are the available run modes in QTP

- ➢ Run
  - Normal
  - Fast
- ➢ Update Run
- ➢ Maintenance Run

27. What is the use of Update Run mode?

Update Run Mode used to update the

- ➢ Test Object Description
- ➢ Checkpoint and output value properties
- ➢ Active Screen Images and Value

28. Explain Maintenance Run Mode?

Maintenance Run mode helps us to maintain tests easily when you get a specific type of failures. The failures are:

- ➢ When object is not identified by QTP
- ➢ When the object is not available in Object Repository
- ➢ When the object is identified by Smart Identification

In these cases using maintenance run mode, we can give the comments in runtime and replace objects in script or add objects to object repository

29. How do you run only current Action?

Go to the Action and Select Automation → Run Current Action

30. How do you run from step?

Keep your cursor at the step from where you want to execute and select Automation → Run from current Step.

31. What is Virtual Object?

A virtual object is defined by user in QuickTest to recognize any area of your application as an object. Virtual objects enable you to record and run tests on objects that are not normally recognized by QuickTest.

For example, suppose you want to record a test on a Web page containing a bitmap that the user clicks. The bitmap contains several different hyperlink areas, and each area opens a different destination page. When you record a test, the Web site matches the coordinates of the click on the bitmap and opens the destination page.

To enable QuickTest to click at the required coordinates during a run session, you can define a virtual object for an area of the bitmap, which includes those coordinates, and map it to the button class. When you run the test, QuickTest clicks the bitmap in the area defined as a virtual object so that the Web site opens the correct destination page.

In the above image Gmail, Images, Blogs and Sites are the links. Assume that QTP does not identify the links on the image; we can define virtual objects to click on each link.

32. Where does virtual object information get saved?

The created virtual objects get stored in <u>QuickTest installation folder\ dat \ VoTemplate</u>

In this folder the Virtual Objects will be stored by its collection name which you can see in

Virtual Object Manager. The extension of this collection is ".VOT"

33. Explain the limitations of virtual objects?

- QuickTest does not support virtual objects for Analog and Low-Level Recordings.
- Not possible to apply a checkpoint on a virtual object
- Only by recording we can add virtual objects
- Not possible to add virtual objects using Object Repository
- Not possible to spy on a virtual object using object spy
- Virtual Objects doesn't support all methods
- QTP may not identify virtual objects on different screen resolutions
- Virtual object uses the properties Name, Height, Width, X, Y which are the properties that has maximum possibilities for frequent change

34. What is Virtual Object Collection and Virtual Object Manager?

Virtual Object Collection is a group of Virtual Objects. Virtual Object Manager is used to Add and Delete Virtual Objects and Collections.

35. What are the object types which can be defined virtually?

The below object types can be defined in QTP

- Object
- Button
- Table
- List
- Checkbox
- Radio Button

36. What is the difference between Test Settings and Tool Options?

Test Settings are to configure a QTP Test. Tool options are the Global Settings to configure QTP.

The Test Settings are temporary and if you configure a test, the settings will not automatically be applied to other tests. Tool Options are permanent and these settings remain same until you change it.

37. How to disable/enable the recognition of Virtual Objects in Record Time?

We can set this in Tools → Options → General Disable Recognition of Virtual Objects

Check or uncheck this option to make disable/enable the recognition of Virtual Objects in Record Time.

38. How do you share the Tool Option Configuration to other Team Members?

Tool Options can be shared by generating a script file which has Tool Options Configuration. Tools → Options → General pane → Click on "Generate Script" button to generate a script for the configured tool settings.

39. I have to capture text from an image. What type of configuration can you do?

To capture text from an image we have to configure OCR Technology. OCR means Optical Character Recognition. This is used to capture text from an image. The configuration should be like below to get text from an image.

Tools → Options→General Text Recognition

In this window, select Text Recognition Mechanism as "First OCR then Windows API" or "Use only OCR" option to recognize text on an image.

To get text from only single block "Select Single Text Block Mode" and to get text from multiple blocks "Select Multiple Text Block Mode"

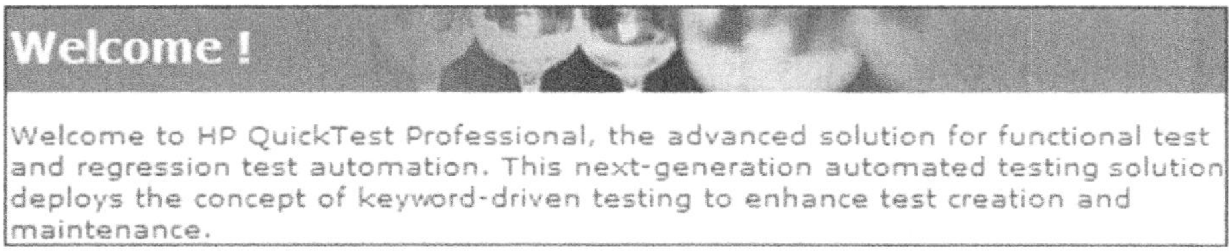

In the above image "Welcome!" is one block and other text is another block. If you select single block, you will get text from only one block. If you select Multiple Block, you will get text from total image.

40. What is the use of Folders pane in Global Options dialog?

A Test can have lot of Resources like Datatables, Object Repositories and Actions ...etc.

When you open the Test, by default, QTP searches for these resources in same Test Folder. If you store the resource files in any other places, then you can add that folder paths in Folders' section to make sure that the Test does not fail because of the modified resource paths.

QTP will first search for resource file in current test path, if not identified, then it will search in all specified folders by priority until the resource is found.

We can add the Folders in Tools → Options → Folders Add folders by clicking on Add (+) button.

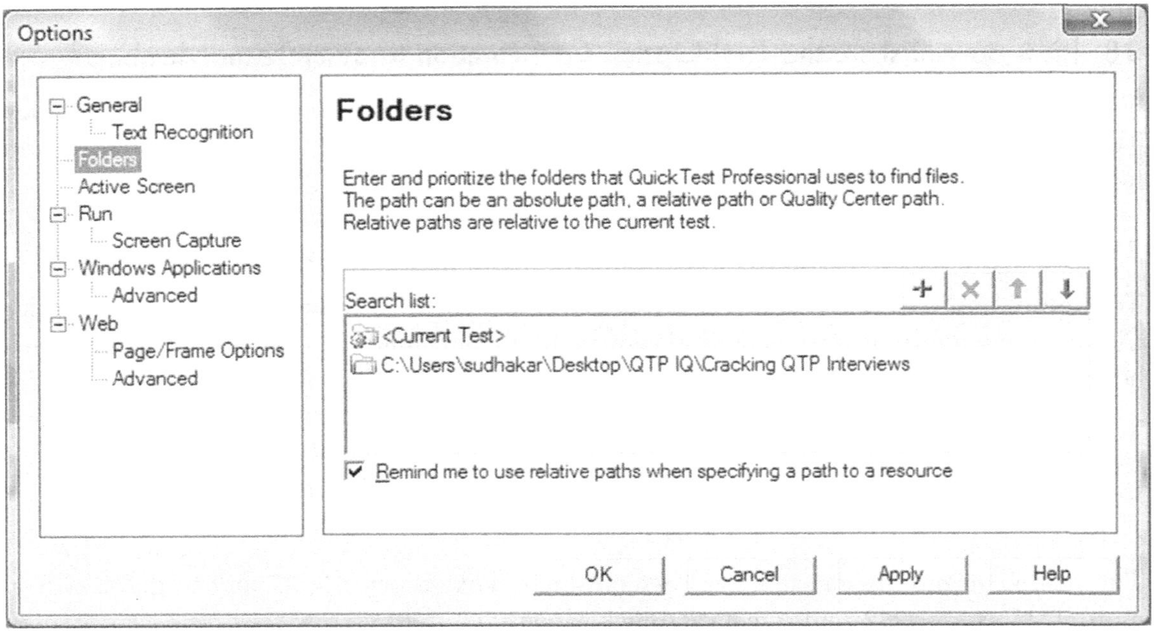

41. What are the types in Active Screen capture levels?

There are four levels

None: Disables capturing of Active Screen files for all applications and Web pages

Minimum: Captures properties only for the recorded object and its parent in the Active Screen of each step. This level saves the original source HTML of all Web pages (prior to dynamic changes) and saves Active Screen files in a compressed format.

Partial: This is a default level. It captures all properties of all objects in the application's active window/dialog box/Web page in the Active Screen of the first step performed in an application's window, plus all properties of the recorded object in subsequent steps in the same window. This level saves Web pages after any dynamic changes and saves Active Screen files in a compressed format.

Complete: Captures all properties of all objects in the application's active window/dialog box/Web page in the Active Screen of each step. This level saves Web pages after any dynamic changes and saves Active Screen files in a compressed format.

42. How do you set Active Screen Levels?

In Tools → Options → Active Screen → Drag level indicator up and down to change Active Screen levels.

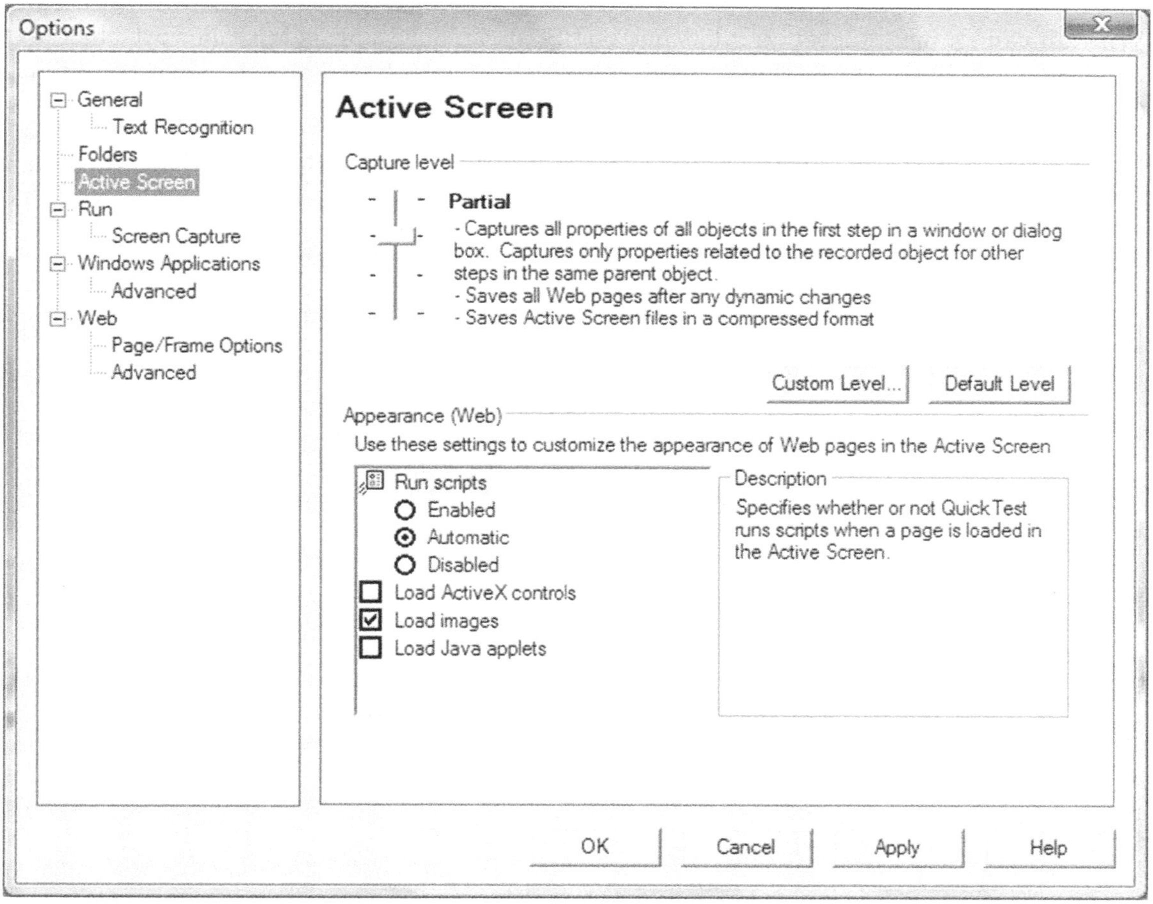

43. How do you configure QTP to run tests from QualityCenter?

In Tools → Options → Run → Select "Allow other HP products to run tests and components" option to run tests from QC.

44. How do you instruct QTP to capture Images on failures?

In Tools → Options → Run → Screen Capture → Select "save still image captures to results" checkbox and select "For Errors" in the list box.

45. I am using windows application. For some of the objects QTP is not capturing Attached Text Property. How do you handle this issue?

Attached text is a property for the objects which cannot have label on it. For example a WinEdit cannot have a label on it like buttons. So it can have a property called attached text. The object can have attached text in any side of the object. Based on that, we can configure QTP to search for attached text in any side of the object.

In the asked scenario, the attached text may be in different side of the object. Because of that, QTP is not capturing Attached Text Property.

We can configure this in Tools → Options → Windows Applications

Here we can set in which side the Attached Text is available for an object. We can also specify Attached Text Search Radius. See the below image.

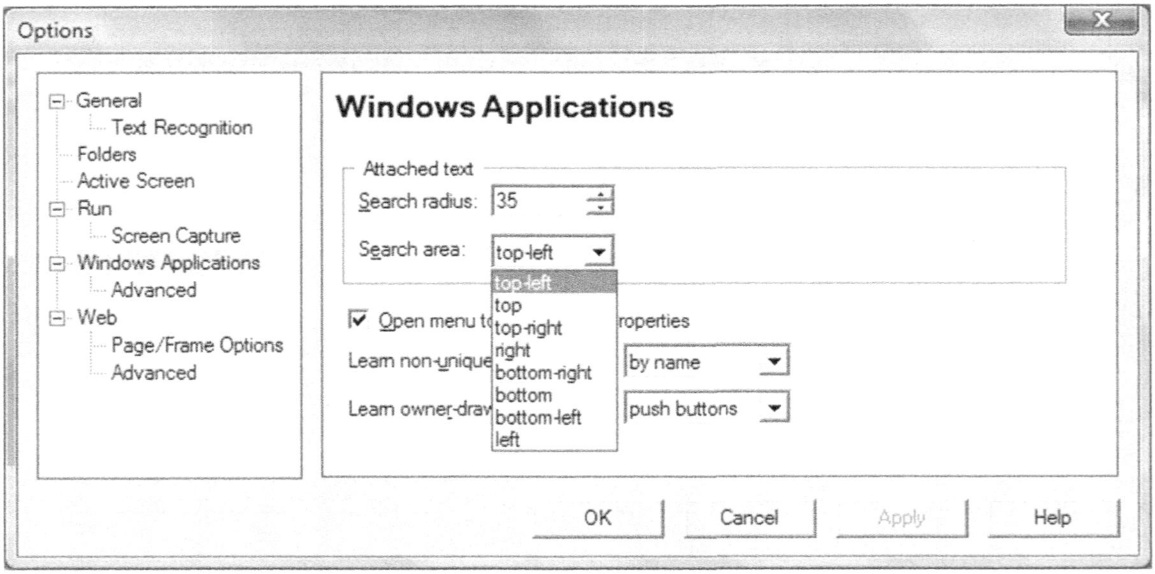

46. How can you ignore QualityCenter in runtime?

In Tools → Options → Web → Select "Ignore Quality Center" option to instruct QTP not to identify QC as the browser or application.

47. How can you configure not to identify a browser in runtime?

In Tools → Options → Web → Add the browsers list by specifying Browser Title and Browser URL.

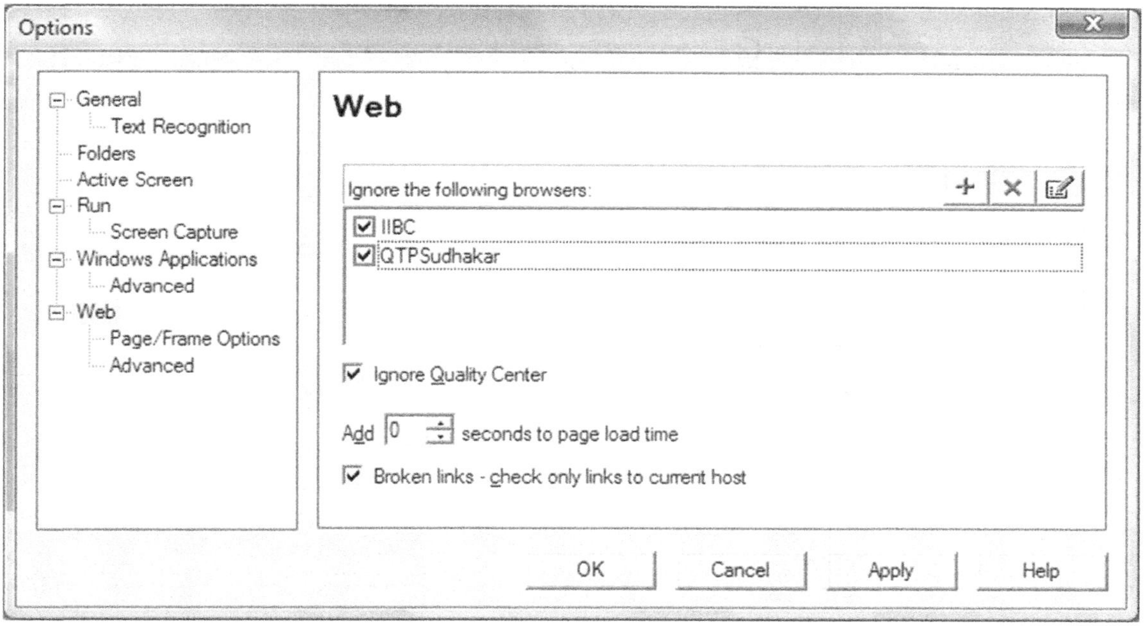

48. When I clicked on a link it displays a popup window. Instead of webbrowser, the window is identified as windows explorer. How to handle the situation?

We can configure QTP to identify a windows explorer as web browser. For this go to

Tools → Options → Web → Advanced → Under Record Settings → Select "Enable Web Support for Microsoft Windows Explorer"

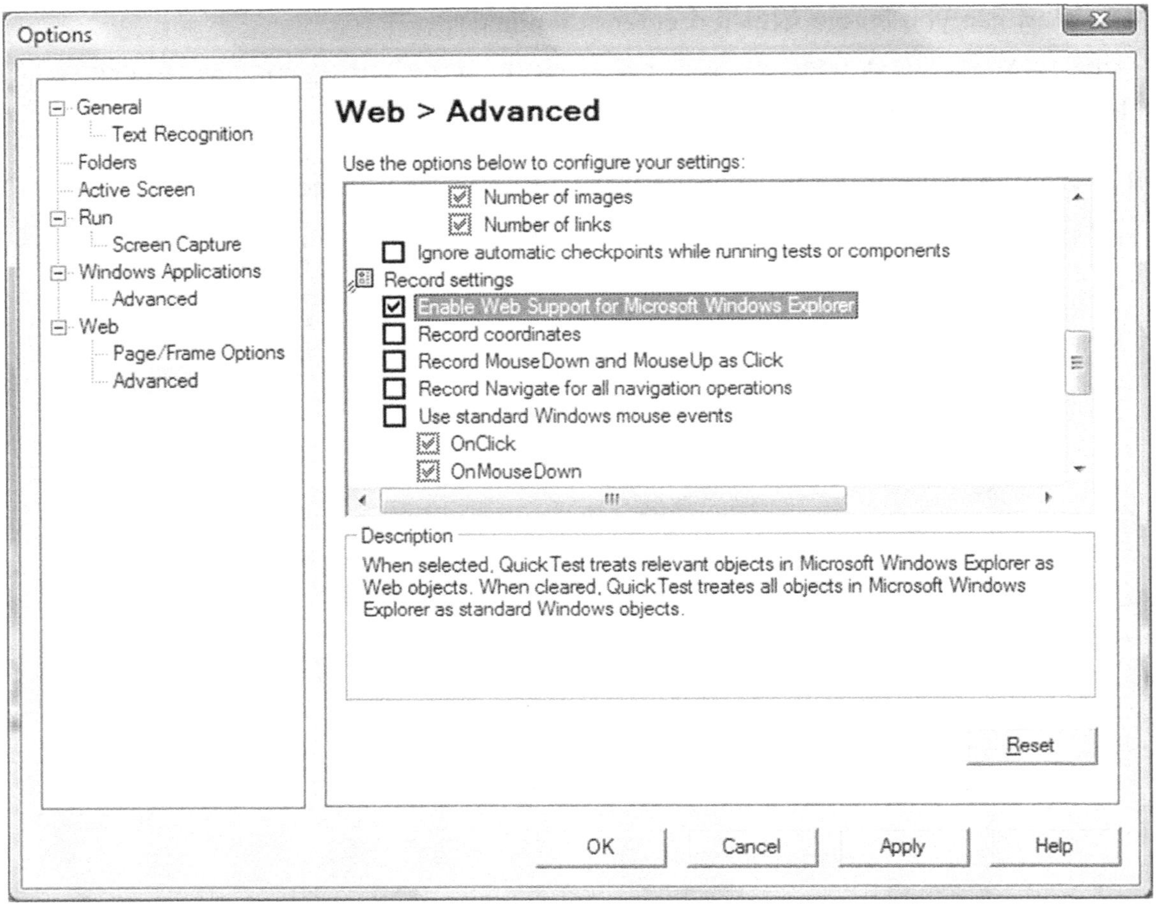
Options
General
Text Recognition
Folders
Active Screen
Run
Screen Capture
Windows Applications
Advanced
Web
Page/Frame Options
Advanced
Web > Advanced
Use the options below to configure your settings:
Number of images
Number of links
Ignore automatic checkpoints while running tests or components
Record settings
Enable Web Support for Microsoft Windows Explorer
Record coordinates
Record MouseDown and MouseUp as Click
Record Navigate for all navigation operations
Use standard Windows mouse events
OnClick
OnMouseDown
Description
When selected, QuickTest treats relevant objects in Microsoft Windows Explorer as Web objects. When cleared, QuickTest treates all objects in Microsoft Windows Explorer as standard Windows objects.
Reset
OK
Cancel
Apply
Help

CHAPTER 11

VBScript

1. How do you open VBScript Help in QTP?

QTP>Help>QuickTestProfessional Help>Contents>VB Script Reference>VB Script>Reference

Purpose of each tab in Help are

Contents – Topic based Tree like browsing

Index - Auto search based on characters typed

Search - String based search

Favorites – Favourite searches added

2. Difference between Variable, String and Keyword

- Variable stores a value.

Example:

i=10

appurl="www.i2brightcareers.com"

In the above *i* and *appurl* are variables.

- String is nothing but set of characters. Ex: "**Welcome To IIBC**". String is usually stored in double quotes.

- ➢ Keyword is a variable which is already used by VBScript. Ex: dim, public, name etc. Variable name in the program should not be a keyword.

3. What is a constant and where do you use?

Constant is a variable whose value CANNOT be changed. Constants are used to define fixed values that cannot be changed during program execution like Application URL, Results folder

4. How will you declare constant?

const RESULTS_FOLDER="D:\MyProject\Automation\Results"

5. How do you differentiate Variables, Strings and Keywords in the Editor?

In QTP editor Variables are in BLACK color, Strings are in RED color and Keywords are in BLUE color.

6. Do we have Data Types in VBScript?

Yes. But we need not to bother about data types while writing VbScript code. System automatically takes care of it.

7. Do we need to declare variables before using in VBScript?

Not required. We can directly start using it. But if we use option explicit at the starting of the program we must declare variable before using them.

8. Is VB Script Object Oriented or Procedure Oriented?

Both

9. Is VB Script Compiled or Interpreted Language?

Interpreted

10. What are different access modifiers available in VBScript?

3 types. Dim, Public, Private

Dim – Entire Program level

Public – Outside Program , Out of class

Private – With in class

11. Output of following code?

```
For i=1 To 10
      i=i+1
      Print(i)
    Next
```

```
O/P ==> 2, 4, 6, 8, 10
```

12. Output of following code?

```
For i=1 To 10 Step 2
        Print(i)
       Next
```

```
O/P ==> 1, 3, 5, 7, 9
```

13. Output of following code?

```
i=1
While i<10
print(i)
Wend
```

```
O/P ==> Infinite loop printing 1 always
```

14. Output of following code?

```
j=2
For i=1 To 3
    While j<4
            Print(i&space(1)&j)
      j=j+1
      Wend
```

```
Next

O/P ==> 1 2

        1 3
```

15. Why Arrays are required?

Arrays store set of values. In VBScript same array can store any data type.

16. What is a Dynamic Array? How do you declare them?

Dynamic arrays are the one whose size is decided during the Program Runtime. Dynamic arrays can be declared using **Redim** keyword. Code is as below:

```
Dim a()

Redim a(10)    ' Declares array with 11 elements

A(0)=10

A(1)=20.5

__

__

A(10)="hello"

Redim a(20)  'Declares array with 21 elements
```

17. Why Keyword Preserve is used?

Preserve Keyword is used to preserve the values in the array elements after re-size. For example, in the above code after ReDim to 20 data in the elements 0-10 will become null. If we use Preserve keyword earlier data will be retained.

Syntax is as follows:
Redim Preserve a(20) 'Declares array with 21 elements including preserving these values

18. Can we declare Multidimensional Arrays in VbScript?

Yes. You can have as many as 60 dimensions. Multiple dimensions can be declared by separating an array's size numbers in the parentheses with commas as depicted in the following example.

Example: *Dim Myarray(5,10)*

Here Myarray is an array variable which is a two-dimensional array consisting of 6 rows and 11 columns

19. What are the inbuilt functions in an Array and their usage?

- **UBound function**

  This will return an integer of the highest subscript or item position in an array.

  Example:

```
Dim myArray(3), arraySize

arraySize = UBound(myArray)+1

                        Print arraySize
```

- **LBound function**

  This will return an integer of the lowest subscript or item position in an array.

  Example:

```
Dim myArray(3), arraySize

arraylbound = LBound(myArray)   'Returns zero

                        Print arraylbound
```

- **Array()**

  An array function takes comma as delimiter and list as its arguments and returns an array to an ordinary variable.

  Example:

```
Dim arrTest

arrTest = Array("elem0","elem1","elem2")
```

- **Isarray**

  This function will return boolean value. True if the variable is an array.

  Example:

```
      Dim a

            a=array("jha",1,1)

check=isarray(a)
```

```
        If check=True Then
                Print "a is an array variable"
    Else
                Print " a is not an array variable"
    End If
```

- **Erase**

  The erase function either reinitializes a fixed array or de-allocates the memory used by a dynamic array. **Write program to print size of an Array**

20. Why do you require Functions/Procedures?

Functions will help to organize my code effectively and also to reuse code

21. How many types of Procedures you have in VB Script?

Two types

- Sub Procedure
- Function Procedure

22. What is the difference between Sub and Function Procedure?

Sub doesn't return a value and Function returns value.

23. How will you reuse functions?

I keep all functions under a Library and call that library in all the programs where ever the function is required.

24. What are parameters in the function?

Parameters are used to pass input values to the function.

25. Is Following code Correct?

```
Function myadd(a,b)
   c=a+b
    return c
```

Ans: No. Two Errors are there.

1. Function must end with End Function.
2. Return statement should not be used to return values

Correct code is

```
Function myadd(a,b)
      c=a+b
      myadd=c
End Function
```

26. What is the output of following code?

```
Sub hello(student)
        Msgbox(student&vbtab&"Welcome To IIBC")
End Sub
r1=hello("Gopal")
Msgbox(r1)
```

Ans: A runtime error will be thrown because, sub procedure never returns a value and code is trying to capture return value.

27. In how many ways can parameters be passed?

- Parameters are passed in two ways. Byval and Byref.
- Byval means changes in called function will not reflect to caller
- Byref means changes in called function will reflect to caller
- By default, parameters are passed as ByRef.

28. What is the output of following code

```
Function myadd(a,b)
   c=a+b
    a=50
    b=100
   myadd=c
```

```
End Function

i1=100

i2=200

r1=myadd(i1,i2)

print(r1)

print(i1)

print(i2)
```

Ans: Output is

```
r1    -    300

i1    -    50

i2    -    100
```

In the above code a,b are ByRef (default). So changed values in function reflects caller. We have change a,b in function hence i1,i2 have taken the changed values.

29. In Following Function Syntax List out

Returns a specified number of characters from a string.

`Mid(string, start[, length])`

- **Function Name**
- **How many Parameters?**
- **Optional Parameters**
- **Mandatory Parameters**
- **Return Type**

Ans:

Function Name	- Mid
How many Parameters?	- 3
Optional Parameters	- length
Mandatory Parameters	- string,start
Return Type	- string (specified number of characters)

30. Print Name of current month (For Example: January)

```
Msgbox(MonthName(Month(Date())))

Or

m=Month(Date())    'm - variable to store month

mn=MonthName(m)  ' mn- variable to store month name

Msgbox(mn)
```

31. How do you print which day is today (For Example: Wednesday)

```
Msgbox(WeekdayName(Weekday(Date())))
```

32. Print current Time

Msgbox(Time)

33. Difference between Date and Now.

Date prints only Date and Now prints both Date and Time

34. Write a function mystrrev to reverse a given string

```
Function mystrrev(str)

      l=Len(str)

revstr=""

      For i=l To 1 step -1

            ch=Mid(str,i,1)

            revstr=revstr&ch

      Next

      mystrrev= revstr

End Function
```

35. What is a Library?

Library is a place holder for Function and Sub Procedures.

36. What is the extension of QTP library file?

In QTP three types of Library extensions are allowed

- .vbs
- .qfl
- .txt

37. How many Functions does a Library contain?

There is no limit. But it is a good practice to categorize related functions in to different libraries.

38. Can Library have both Sub and Function Procedures?

Yes. It can.

39. What is the purpose of Keyword *Option Explicit*?

Option Explicit forces the declaration of variables before their usage.

40. What is the purpose of Keyword *On Error Resume Next*?

On Error Resume Next is a VBScript statement that instructs QTP to go to next line even though there is an error in the current line.

41. What is the purpose of Keyword *Err.Clear and Err.Number*?

Err.clear -	clears the error in the Err object
Err.Number -	displays the numerical value of the error present in the Err object
Err.Description-	displays the description of the error present in the Err object

42. Check whether the string is a PALINDROME

```
Dim str,revStr

str= inputbox("Enter the String")

print(" The Given String is :   " +str)

revStr = StrReverse(str)

If StrComp(str,revStr) = 0 Then
```

```
      print(" The Given String is a Palindrome")
else
      print(" The Given String is not a Palindrome ")
End If
```

43. Check Given Number is a Prime?

```
N1=inputbox("Enter the starting number")
     flag=0
     For i=2 to N1-1
        If (N1 mod i) = 0 Then
            flag=1
            Exit for
        End If
     Next
    If flag=0 Then
Print("Prime")
Else
      Print("Not Prime")
         End If
```

44. Print all values from an Array

```
Dim inputArray, index
inputArray=array(10,"20.5","IIIBC","QTP","Siva")
    print("Elements of inputArray are")
For index=lbound(inputArray) to ubound(inputArray)
    print(inputArray(index ))
Next
```

45. What are the naming Restriction you have in VBScript variables declaration?

Variable names follow the standard rules for naming anything in VBScript. A variable name:

- Must begin with an alphabetic character.
- Cannot contain a period.
- Must not exceed 255 characters.
- Must be unique in the scope in which it is declared.

46. What an Exit Statement will do?

If user wants to exit the procedure when certain conditions are met; exit statements can be used within the procedure. Exit statements when encountered within a procedure body, the procedure exits unconditionally.

Syntax: Exit [Procedure]

47. How will you add library to QTP Script?

To add library files created above to QTP follow the steps below:

1. Select **File>Settings>Resources**. Test Settings Dialog will open.

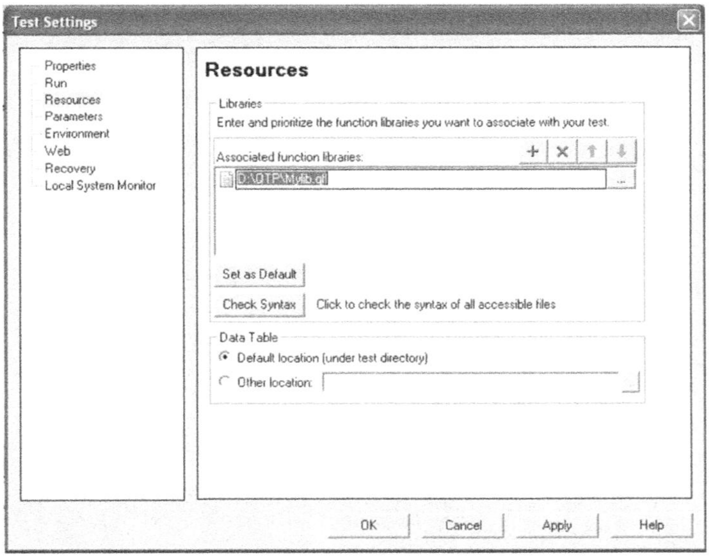

2. Click + to add a library file. A file browse button will be displayed.
3. Click on browse button and select the file.

4. Automatic Relative Path conversion dialog appears. Select Yes to close the Automatic Relative Path dialog and click OK to close the Test Settings Dialog.
5. Click Check Syntax button to validate the syntax of functions in the library file.

48. Name few important String Functions?

Function	Description
Len	Returns the number of characters in a string
Mid	Returns a specified number of characters from a string
InStr	Returns the position of the first occurrence of one string within another. The search begins at the first character of the string
InStrRev	Returns the position of the first occurrence of one string within another. The search begins at the last character of the string
LCase	Converts a specified string to lowercase
UCase	Converts a specified string to uppercase
Left	Returns a specified number of characters from the left side of a string
Right	Returns a specified number of characters from the right side of a string
LTrim	Removes spaces on the left side of a string
RTrim	Removes spaces on the right side of a string
Trim	Removes spaces on both the left and the right side of a string
Replace	Replaces a specified part of a string with another string a specified number of times
Space	Returns a string that consists of a specified number of spaces
StrComp	Compares two strings and returns a value that represents the result of the comparison
String	Returns a string that contains a repeating character of a specified length
StrReverse	Reverses a string

49. How do you print Tab space?

Constant **VbTab** can be used to print a Tab Space.

Example:

```
Print("Author:" & VbTab & "Siva")
```

In the output we can see a Tab space between Author and Siva

50. How do you print 10 spaces?

Function *space* can be used to print a space

Example:

```
Print("Author:" & Space(10) & "Siva")
```

In the output we can see 10 spaces between Author and Siva

51. What is the purpose of *string* function?

String function Returns a string that contains a repeating character of a specified length.

Example:

```
Print(string(5,"*"))
```

`Prints * character for 5 times (*****)`

52. Difference between Eval and Execute functions?

In VBScript, $x = y$ can be interpreted in two ways. The first is as an assignment statement, where the value of y is assigned to x. The second interpretation is as an expression that tests if x and y have the same value. The **Eval** method always uses the second interpretation, whereas the **Execute** statement always uses the first.

53. What is the purpose of ExecuteFile statement?

The **ExecuteFile** statement makes all functions, subroutines available to the action without associating function library to the QTP test.

Note: You cannot debug a file that is called using an **ExecuteFile** statement, or any of the functions contained in the file. In addition, when debugging a test that contains an **ExecuteFile** statement, the execution marker may not be correctly displayed. These problems can be handled by using LoadLibrary statement.

CHAPTER 12

Debugging

1. What is Debugging?

Debugging is the process of locating errors in computer program. By debugging you can identify and handle problems in your tests, function libraries, and registered user functions.

2. Have you got involved in Debugging?

Yes. I have got involved in debugging QTP automation scripts written in VBScript using the debugging option provided in QTP. Many a times, I have used debugger because I have to enhance existing scripts for minor updations in the application.

3. Is Debugging a job of developer or Tester?

If we are talking about the debugging of the code developed for an application, then it must be done by the developer. If we are talking about the debugging of the automation scripts developed by Automation Tester, then tester must debug.

4. You can use print statement to display errors and correct them? Why do you need debugger?

I agree that print statement is a good option for small programs within 50 lines of code. But for large programs, a debugger is always a good choice. More over you can change the values of program variables during run time.

5. What is a Break point?

Break Points are used to break the script execution. After script execution is stopped, you can run the script line by line.

6. How do you insert Break Point?

This can be achieved in two ways.

1. To apply a breakpoint, click a line in your test where you need break point and Choose **Debug > Insert/Remove Breakpoint**

7. Can I have multiple break points within the same program?

Yes. You can have as many break points as you want.

8. How do you Remove Break Point?

This can be achieved in three ways.

1. To remove a single breakpoint, click a line in your test or component with the breakpoint symbol and Choose **Debug > Insert/Remove Breakpoint**
2. To remove all breakpoints, choose **Debug > Clear All Breakpoints**

9. How will I run script line by line?

We can use *Debug>Step Over* (F10) to go through line by line. For example if a line contains function like Multiply to go into the function and debug we can use *Debug>Step Into* (F11) and at any point of time we can come out of the function we can use *Debug>Step Out* (Shift + F11)

10. How will you run line by line with in the function?

We can use *Step Over* (F10) to go through line by line once we have entered into function using *Step Into* (F11)

11. Can I insert break point within the procedure?

Yes. You can insert break point even in the procedure.

12. What is a Debug Viewer?

Debug viewer is used to view the values of variables, and to watch the results of expression and also to execute commands.

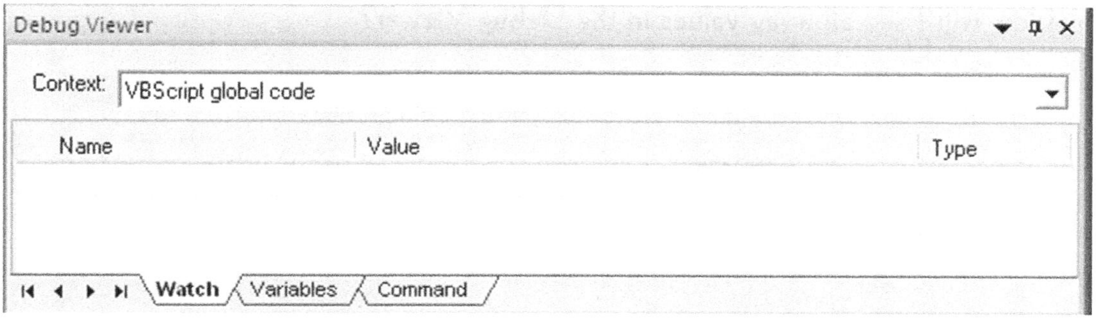

- **Watch** tab: Displays the current values and types of variables and VBScript expressions that you add to the Watch tab, and enables you to modify the values of displayed variables and properties.
- **Variables** tab: Displays the current values and types of all variables in the main script of the current action, or in a selected subroutine, and enables you to modify their values.
- **Command** tab: Enables you to run VBScript commands in your paused run session.

13. I want to see how the value of variable x is getting changed time to time. What should I do?

Add variable x to watch tab

14. I can even see variables using Variables Tab. Then why should I use Watch Tab?

- Yes you can do that. But Variables Tab shows all the variable values in the program. For example if you have 50 variables in the program all will be shown. Out of them monitoring one variable closely is little difficult. So it is a good practice to add it to watch tab.
- If you want to see expression values like x+y you can, because it is possible only in watch tab

15. Why is Command prompt used?

You can execute any command with this Tab. For example if current value of variable x is 100 you want to change it to 500. Go to command Tab and type x=500. Now the new value of x will become 500. You can see this updated value either in variables Tab or Watch Tab.

16. How will I see all array values in the Debug Viewer?

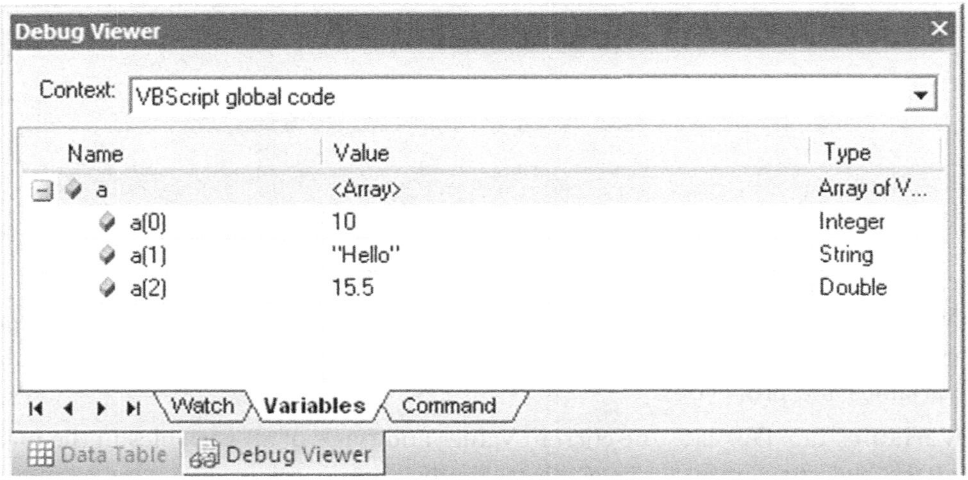

Above diagram shows How Array values are displayed in the debug viewer.

17. What happens if I click Run button after halting a program at a break point?

Program will continue to execute until next break point is encountered or end of program has been reached.

18. Do you get debugger along with QTP?

No. You have to install **Microsoft Script Debugger** to run tests in debug mode. If it is not installed, you can use the QuickTest Additional Installation Requirements Utility to install it:

Select **Start > All Programs > QuickTestProfessional > Tools > Additional Installation Requirements**.

19. Did you face any limitations with Debugger?

- If a library is loaded using an **ExecuteFile** statement, you cannot debug the file or any of the functions contained in the library and execution marker may not be displayed correctly.
- When you open a test present in Quality Center project, QTP creates a local copy of the external resources. Therefore, any changes you apply to any external resource

that is saved in your Quality Center project, such as a function library, will not be recognized in the test until the test is closed and reopened.

20. Can you temporarily disable break points without removing them?

Yes. If you want to run the entire script and see the output without stopping at break points, you can disable them using **Debug>Enable/Disable All break points**

CHAPTER 13

Windows and Web Objects

1. Difference between Class and Object?

- Class is a blue print. Objects are the instances/ real existing elements of the class
- Every Object must belong to one class

2. Identify Objects and Classes in the Following line?

```
Browser("BookStore").Page("Home").Weblist("Category").select "Testing"

Browser("BookStore").Page("Home").WebEdit("Title").set "QTP"
```

Ans: Objects – Bookstore,Home,Category,Title

Classes – Browser,Page,Weblist,WebEdit

3. Difference between Method and Function

Method is always associated with Object and Function is not associated with any object.

In the following code

Browser("BookStore").Page("Home").Weblist("Category").select "Testing"

Browser("BookStore").Page("Home").WebEdit("Title").set "QTP"

select,set are methods

Few examples of Functions are Mid,Len, Left,CInt

4. How do you know methods present in an object?

Two ways

- I can use help file. For example to find methods in WebButton Objects I have to do following

  QTP>Help>Quicktest Professional Help> HP QuickTest Professional Object Model Reference>Web>Web Button

- I can use InteliScense editor of QTP which gives me all methods supported by object after typing dot(.) next to object.

  First one is always better approach since you can find lots of documentation for each method

5. Is the following code correct to enter QTP into Web Edit box named Title?

```
Browser("BookStore").Page("Home").WebEdit("Title").enter "QTP"
```

Ans: No. WebEdit doesn't have a method called enter

6. Can you write code for logging into gmail?

```
Browser("Gmail").Page("Login").WebEdit("Username").set  "testuser"

Browser("Gmail").Page("Login").WebEdit("Password").setsecure
"4cf74fec5771be34dd6458c36ed75307cf0fea5a52bb"

Browser("Gmail").Page("Login").WebButton("SignIn").click

If Browser("Gmail").Page("Inbox").Exist Then

      Print("Login successful")

Else

      Print("Login Failed")

End If
```

Note: Do not forget to write the code which will check whether page is existing or not. It is very essential to check whether inbox page opened or not using **exist** property

7. Do we have any way to reduce the lengthy lines of the script?

Yes. You have two different ways to achieve this.

Simple way is to use **with** statement. With Browser ("BookStore").Page("Home")

```
.WebList("Category").select "Testing"

.WebEdit("Title").set "QTP"

.WebButton("search").click

   End With
```

Please observe the dot (.) before each line with in with statement which is mandatory

Second way is assigning to a variable as follows

```
set x=Browser ("BookStore").Page("Home")

x.WebList("Category").select "Testing"

x.WebEdit("Title").set "QTP"

x.WebButton("search").click
```

In the above code you are storing Page object and its entire parent hierarchy in a variable 'x'. This object is further used to code with objects present in the Page.

8. How do you capture an image of Yahoo Home Page?

```
Browser ("Yahoo").Page("Home").CaptureBitmap "D:\CrackQTPInterviews\
yahoohome.bmp"
```

9. Difference between check and Check Property

Check is a method that is created for each check point which we apply like Standard, Bitmap etc... Check Property is used to check only one property of an object. For example if we want to check whether WebButton SignIn is disabled, the coding is as follows:

```
r=Browser("Gmail").Page("Login").WebButton("SignIn").
CheckProperty("disabled",1)

If r=TRUE Then

      print("SignIn Button is disabled")

Else
```

```
    print("SignIn Button is enabled")
End If
```

10. How do I know what are the properties supported by an object?

Use **Tools > Object Spy** and spy the object. Select radio button *Identification Properties* and Tab Properties. You will see all the properties supported by the object as shown below.

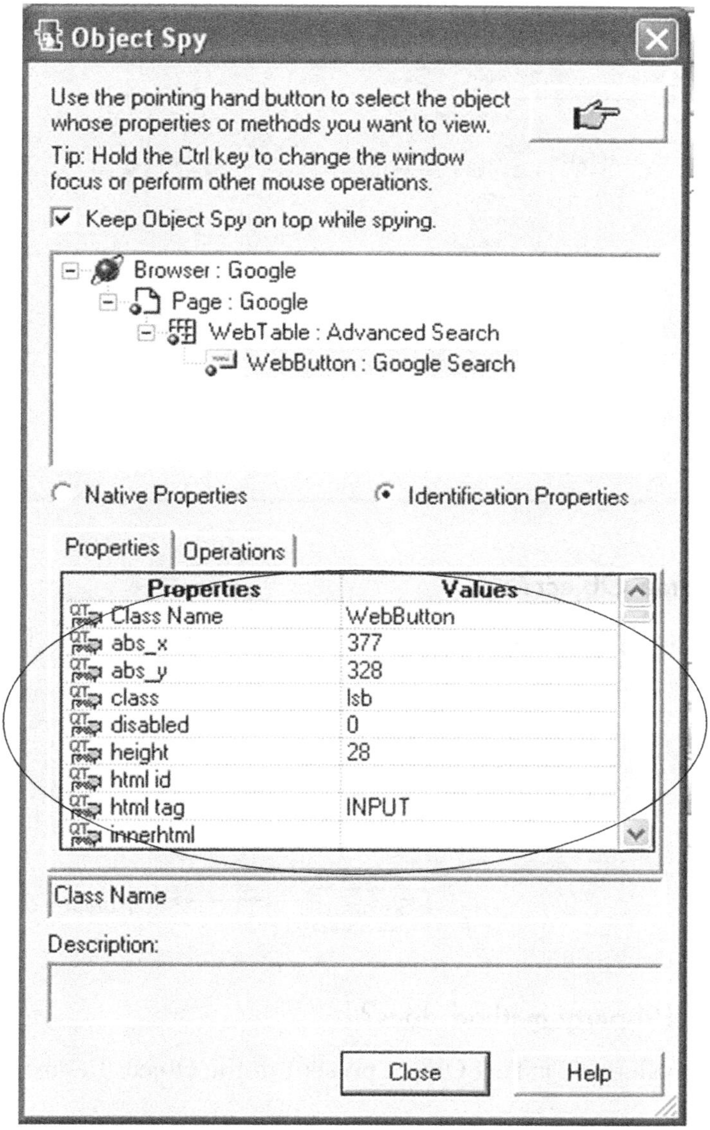

11. What is a Test Object?

Object used in the Script i.e., Object present in the Object Repository

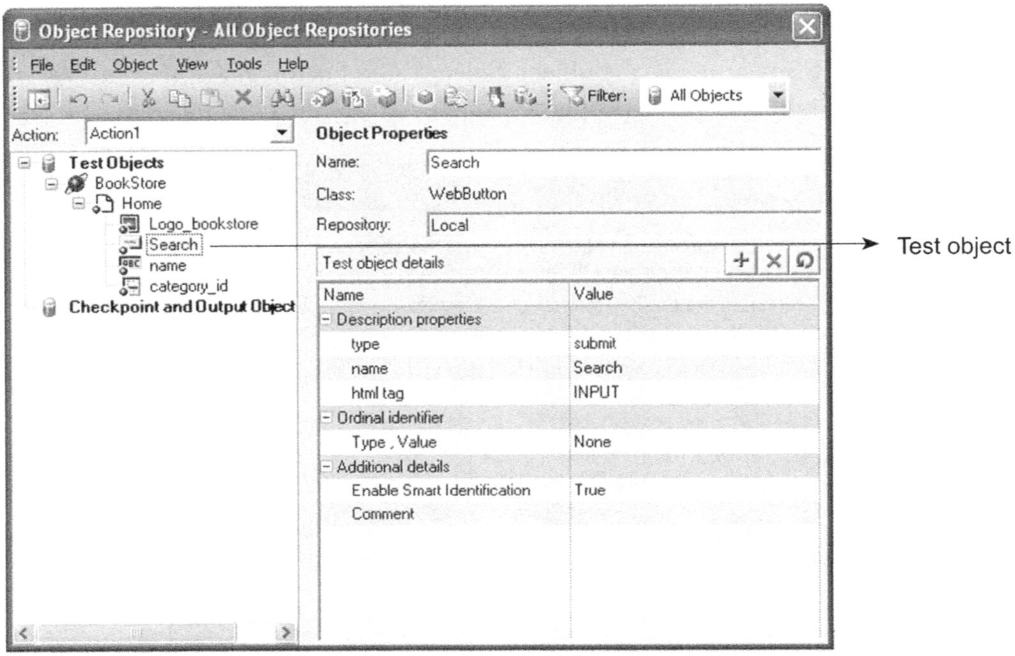

12. What is Runtime Object?

Object Present in the Application. Observe below for example for Test Object and RunTime Object.

13. What GetTOProperty method does?

Reads the property values of a Test Object present in the Object Repository.

14. How do you know which are the properties you can read with GetROProperty?

Use object spy and spy the object. Select radio button "Identification Properties" and Tab Properties. You will see all the properties that can be read using GetROProperty.

15. Difference between GetTOProperty Vs GetROProperty

GetTOProperty returns the value from the test object's description. **GetROProperty** returns the current property value of the object in the application during the test run. You can use the **GetTOProperty** method to retrieve the values of only those properties that are included in the test object description.

For example WebButton **Google Search** present in Object repository as shown below has only three identification properties type, html tag and name in object repository. By using **GetTOProperty** we can retrieve only these three properties.

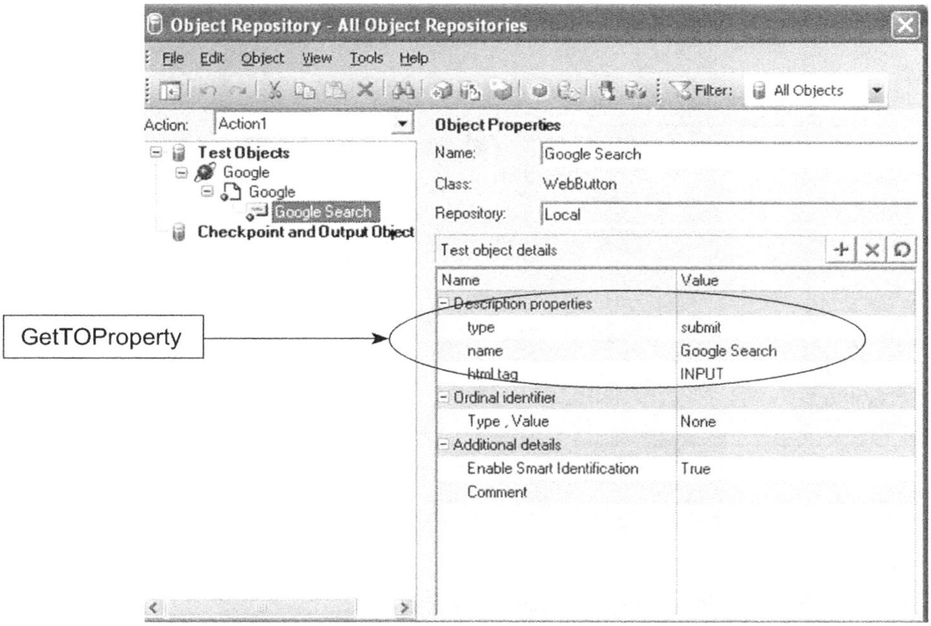

Whereas **GetROProperty** is used to retrieve any of the Identification properties of test object shown by Object spy. In below diagram we can find many Identification properties for Google Search Object like Class Name, abs_x, abs_y. To retrieve any of those identification properties displayed by Object Spy we will use **GetROProperty.**

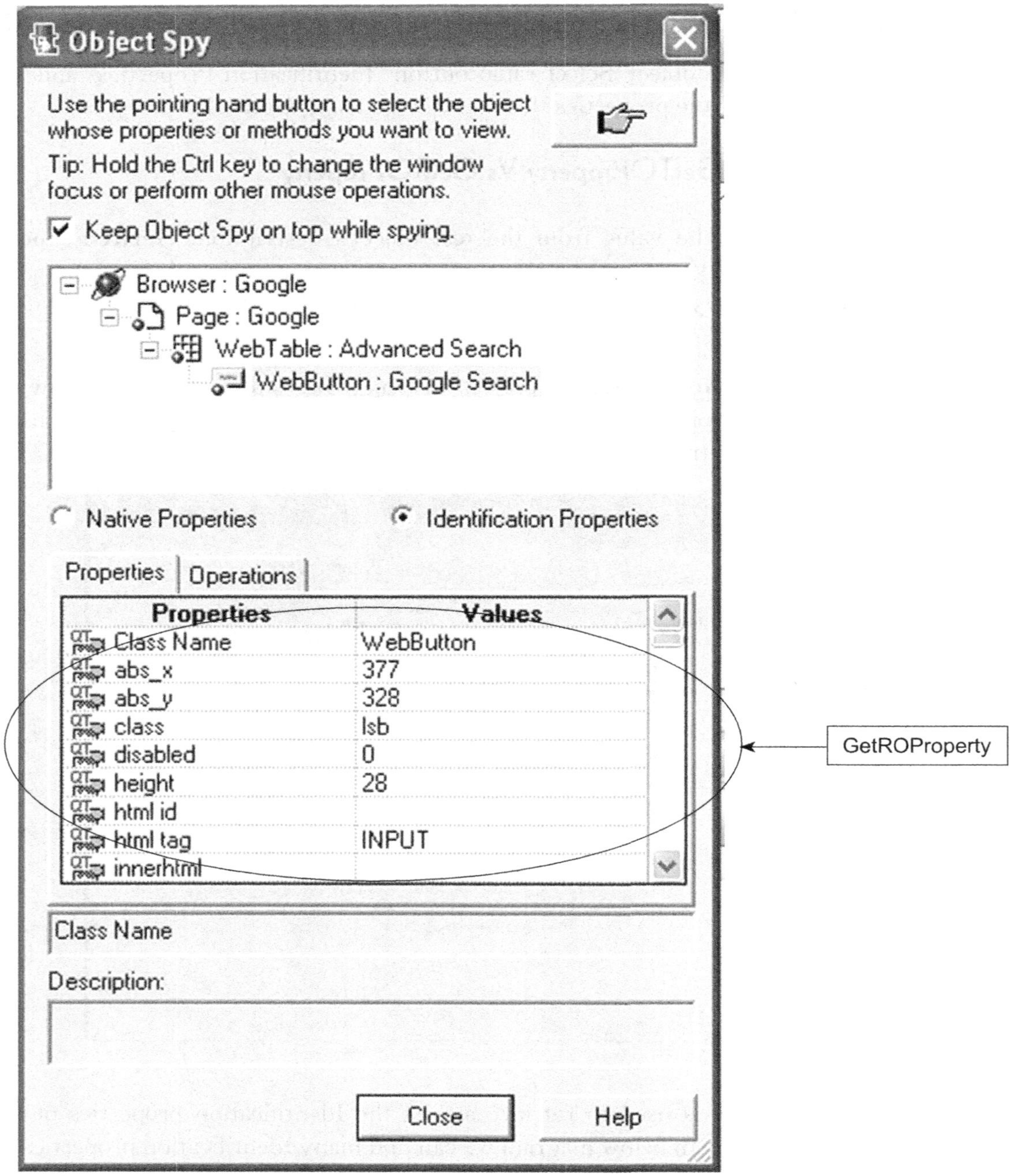
Object Spy
Use the pointing hand button to select the object whose properties or methods you want to view.
Tip: Hold the Ctrl key to change the window focus or perform other mouse operations.
Keep Object Spy on top while spying.
Browser : Google
Page : Google
WebTable : Advanced Search
WebButton : Google Search
Native Properties
Identification Properties
Properties
Operations
Properties
Values
Class Name
WebButton
abs_x
377
abs_y
328
class
lsb
disabled
0
height
28
html id
html tag
INPUT
innerhtml
Class Name
Description:
Close
Help
GetROProperty

16. Can we Read Number of items present in the Web List?

Yes. Using property **items count** we can achieve this.

17. How do you write Automation Script to check number of characters allowed by Web Edit Box?

Property value **max length** will return maximum number of characters allowed to enter in Edit Box. This property value can be read by GetROProperty method.

18. What is the difference between width in Characters and Max length properties of Web Edit box?

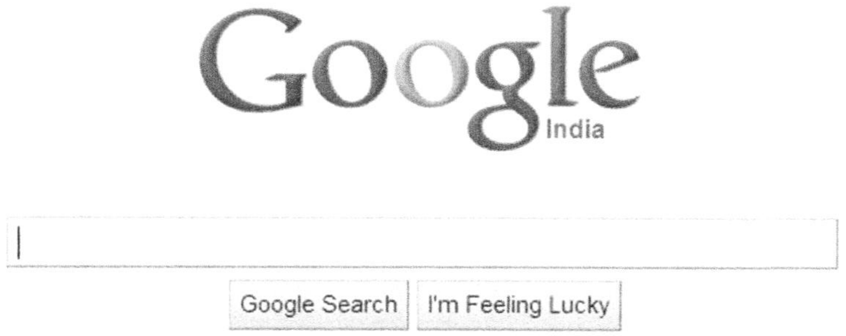

Width in characters property gives the width of the Edit box in terms of number of characters. **max length** property will give how many maximum characters we can enter in Edit box. For example in the above Google Search Edit box **width in characters** property will return 57 indicating that edit box can display maximum 57 characters to user. Whereas **max length** property returns a value 2048 indicating user can enter string of maximum length 2048 characters for search.

19. What is the difference between width and width in characters properties?

Width will return the width of object in terms of number of pixels, **width in characters** returns the width in terms of number of allowed characters.

20. Write the code to Read items count of WebList Category?

```
ic=Browser("BookStore").Page("Home").WebList("Category").
GetROProperty("items count")
```

21. What is the difference between value and name property of WebButton Search?

Name property represents the name given by the developer to identify the button. Value gives the text displayed on the web button. For example, the developer can give a name as HomeSearch and the text displayed on the button as search. As a user, we see the button with name search and developer identifies it during his coding as HomeSearch

22. Write the code to Read the text displayed on WebButton Search?

```
btnText=Browser("BookStore").Page("Home").WebButton("search").
GetROProperty("Value")
```

23. Write the code to Read width of WebList Category and also check whether it is equivalent to 20?

```
wdth=Browser("BookStore").Page("Home").WebList("Category").
GetROProperty("width")

if wdth=20 then

      Msgbox("Width is Correct")

Else

      Msgbox('Width is incorrect")

End If
```

24. How do you read Default Value present in a WebEdit box?

This can be achieved by Reading property **default value.** Similarly we can read default value for Web List also.

25. Difference between Value and Default Value properties?

Value always returns the present value in the object. Default value always returns the value that was present in the object when page was freshly loaded.

For example in Google registration page, when page is opened, default country shown is India and you changed it to UK. Now if I use GetROProperty method; **value** property returns UK and **default value** property returns India. Assume if you haven't changed the country name, then both will return same.

26. What is a FireEvent Method?

FireEvent Method Triggers various events on web objects like onchange, onclick, ondblClick, onmouseover, onmouseout, onmouseup, onmousedown

27. What is the difference between click and Fireevent onclick ?

Both do the same.

28. Then why are two options provided?

Fireevent triggers many events other than onclick like ondblclick, onmouseover, onmouseout, onmouseup, onmousedown. Manytimes we can observe that web application depicts different behaviors when we are moving the mouse over the objects. Since click is a commonly used method of the WebButton it was included as an additional method in the list of methods supported by WebButton.

29. I have used onmouseover event of FireEvent method on a link, WebButton, WebEdit box etc. But I didn't find any event on the application. Why?

Using these events is relevant only when developers write the corresponding handlers for an object. For example if the developer has not written any mouseover handler for a button, then even though you fire mouseover event using FireEvent method there is no difference that you can find in the application.

30. I have used drag and drop method to drag and drop a web button search. But nothing happened. Why?

Drag and Drop method should be used only on applications/objects that supports the drag and drop operation. Drag and Drop operation has to be enabled while designing the application. Since application object you have worked is not supporting Drag n Drop, your QTP methods of Drag and Drop cannot do anything. A simple way to understand this concept is observe whether you can drag and drop search button manually. If manually it is possible it is also possible to do drag and drop through QTP automation. Otherwise if you cannot do drag manually you cannot do it through QTP also.

31. How do you get link color?

We can parse for color attribute by reading OuterHtml property using GetROProperty.

32. When I am adding a Link to Object Repository it is identifying as WebElement Object. Why?

You have to observe that above Web Element object also has a Link object. You must select that.

33. How do you know columns present in a web Table?

Web Table has cols (Columns) property which can be used to read the names of all columns.

34. How do you select multiple items in a list box?

To select multiple items first the WebList object you are using must support multiple items selection. I mean while designing List box developer decides whether to allow single selection or Multi selection. For example your age list box should allow selection of only one value and Places you like can allow multiple items selection.

Assuming developer has allowed multiple items selection, then you have to use following code syntax to select multiple items.

```
Browser("BookStore").Page("Home").WebList("Category").select "All"

Browser("BookStore").Page("Home").WebList("Category").ExtendSelect
"Databases"

Browser("BookStore").Page("Home").WebList("Category").ExtendSelect
"Testing"
```

Observe the *ExtendSelect* method which is used for selecting multiple items.

35. How do you select second item in the list box?

We can use position of the item as input value to select method and we can select second item. This can be done in two ways

Using Position Number

Example Syntax

```
Browser("BookStore").Page("Home").WebList("Category").select 1
```

Using # and Position Number

Example Syntax

```
Browser("BookStore").Page("Home").WebList("Category").select "#1"
```

Note: Please observe that you must give double-quotes if you use # and index starts from 0

36. When I read image type property few are showing plain image and few are showing image link. Why?

Plain image is just an image. Clicking on that will not have any effect. Image link is an image with the behavior of link. By clicking on image link we can go to next page referred by image link.

37. How can you find whether web Table has border or not?

Webtable has border property for this

38. How do you know number of Rows present in web table?

We can get number of rows using GetRowCount method. Syntax is

```
rowCount=Browser("BookStore").Page("Home").WebTable("Books").RowCount()
```

39. Is Following Code Correct to get number of Columns in a WebTable?

```
colCount=Browser("BookStore").Page("Home").WebTable("Books").
ColumnCount()
```

Ans: No. ColumnCount method must be applied on per row basis. This is because all rows in a WebTable may not have same number of Columns. For example in below webtable different rows have different columns.

<table>
<tr><td colspan="4"></td></tr>
<tr><td colspan="2"></td><td colspan="2"></td></tr>
<tr><td colspan="2"></td><td colspan="2"></td></tr>
<tr><td></td><td></td><td></td><td></td></tr>
<tr><td></td><td></td><td></td><td></td></tr>
</table>

40. Which property you have to read entire row data in a WebTable?

Unfortunately no direct property to read entire Row Data. You must read cell by cell by using GetCellData method. Anyhow you can append all these cell values and form a row data.

41. Is following code correct to read data from 6th column?

```
cd=Browser("BookStore").Page("Home").WebTable("Books").GetCellData(6)
```

Ans: No. GetCellData requires mandatorily Row Number and Column Name. Correct syntax is

```
cd=Browser("BookStore").Page("Home").WebTable("Books").
GetCellData(row,col)
```

where row, col are variable that contain row number and column number

42. How do you find through automation whether list and edit boxes of below are left aligned?

Ans: I can just read abs_x property of both objects. If it is same they are left aligned.

43. What is the difference between two properties x and abs_x?

x is always measured as the distance from top left corner of parent object. abs_x is always measured the distance from Top Left corner of the Screen.

44. Write Code to check whether link Advanced Search Exists in the Web page?

```
If Browser("BookStore").Page("Home").Link("Advanced Search").Exist Then
      Msgbox("Advanced Search Link Exists")
      Else
            Msgbox("Advanced Search Link Doesn't exist")
      End If
```

45. I have clicked on a link. I want QTP script to wait until the WebPage loaded. What should I do?

Ans: Use Sync method. Coding Syntax is

```
Browser("BookStore").Page("Home").Link("Advanced Search").click
Browser("BookStore").Page("AdvSearch").sync
```

—

—

Sync method makes the script to wait until the page is fully loaded.

46. What is the difference between Exist and Sync method?

Both are entirely different. Exist method will tell you whether the object is available in the page or not. It just returns true if the object is available else returns false. Sync will wait until the page is fully loaded.

47. How will you Navigate to a particular URL of the application?

Ans: Browser("IIBC").Navigate("www.iibceducation.com") will Navigatenavigate to Home page of IIBC. To go to placements page you can write code as Browser("IIBC").Navigate(www.iibceducation.com/placments.aspx)

Note: The above Navigate method will not start browser. It will only goes from one page to another page within the opened browser.

48. How will you close all tabs in a browser?

We can use CloseAlltabs method of the browser. This closes all tabs in the browser and also the browser.

49. How will you close one tab in a browser?

Ans: We can use close method of the browser

50. How do you check whether two tabs in the same or different browsers are siblings?

Ans: You can use **IsSiblingTab** method of Browser Object.

51. How do you click Backward,Forward,Refresh,Stop buttons of Browser?

QTP has provided relevant methods **Backward, Forward, Refresh, Stop** for browser object to achieve this.

52. How do you know the version of the browser you are using?

QTP has provided a property **application version** which returns the version of the Browser we are using.

53. How do you get the Title of the web page?

You can use title property of the page object.

```
pgttl=Browser("BookStore").Page("Home").GetROProperty("title")
```

54. How do you Automate a Requirement of Browsing a File?

WebFile Object can be used to automate file browsing operations that can be done by a File Browse (An edit box with a browse button attached, used to select a file from the File dialog box) object.

Code Syntax to automate attaching a file is

```
Browser("Goole").Page("ComposeMail").WebFile"D:\IIBC\InterviewQuestions.
pdf"
```

55. Write code to select a radio button named Firefox from the following?

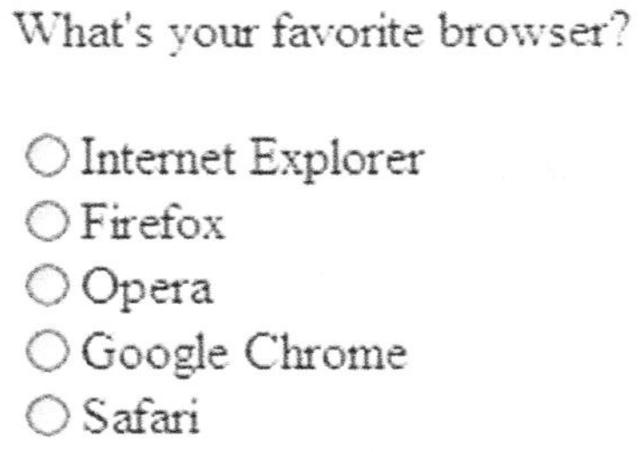


```
Browser("Prefrences").Page("UserPref").WebRadioGroup("BrowserChoice").
select "Firefox"
```

OR

```
Browser("Prefrences").Page("UserPref").WebRadioGroup("BrowserChoice").
select "#1"
```

OR

```
Browser("Prefrences").Page("UserPref").WebRadioGroup("BrowserChoice").
select 1
```

56. How will you start IE browser through Automation Program?

This is possible by using Run method of Systemutil object. Following is code syntax

```
Systemutil.Run "C:\Program Files\Internet Explorer\iexplore.exe"
```

57. How will you start Notepad through Automation Program?

```
Systemutil.Run "Notepad.exe"
```

58. How will you close process using its title?

```
Systemutil.CloseProcessByWndTitle "Title of Window"
```

CHAPTER 14

Utility Objects

1. How are Utility Objects different from Web Objects?

Web objects are used only in applications developed with Web Technology where as Utility Objects are used in applications developed with any Technology. Otherwise Utility objects are not specific to any technology; they are commonly used in all technologies.

2. Can you name few of the utility objects you are familiar with?

Crypt, Report Event, DataTable, DTSheet, DTParameter, Extern, Environment, Recovery, Repositories Collection

3. What is the Purpose of Crypt Object?

Crypt Object is used to encrypt the password

4. How do you encrypt the password entered in the Password Field?

Encrypt method of crypt object will encrypt the password. Syntax is

```
e_passwd=Crypt.Encrypt("PasswordText")
```

5. How do you report Pass or Fail of Step to Test Results?

Pass and Fail status of a step can be reported to results file by using **Reporter.ReportEvent**. Reporter is an object and ReportEvent is a method used to report to result file.

Syntax: **Reporter.ReportEvent EventStatus, ReportStepName, Details**

EventStatus could be

0 or **micPass**: Step Passed

1 or **micFail**: Step Failed

2 or **micDone**: Step Completed. Doesn't matter Passed or Failed

3 or **micWarning**: Step Passed but with some errors.

6. What is an Environment Variable?

Environment Variable defines execution environment of the software. Just like PATH in windows environment even QTP also has some environment variables.

7. How do you Read Environment Variables?

You can set or retrieve the value of environment variables using the Environment object. You can retrieve the value of any environment variable but you can set the value of only user-defined, environment variables.

To set the value of a user-defined, environment variable:

Environment (*VariableName*) = *NewValue*

Or

Environment.Value(*VariableName*) = *NewValue*

Example: Author is the user defined environment variable and we can assign new value for it as shown below.

Environment ("Author")="Siva"

Or

Environment.Value("Author")="Siva"

To retrieve the value of a loaded environment variable:

CurrValue = Environment (*VariableName*)

Or

CurrValue =Environment.Value(*VariableName*)

Example: Below code retrieves built-in environment variable OS from the system.

```
OperSys=Environment("OS")
Msgbox(OperSys)
```

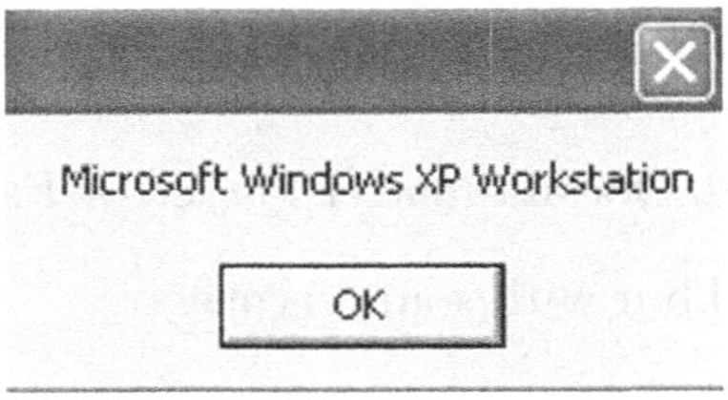

8. How do you write code to load external Environment File?

Environment.LoadFromFile("D:\QTP\Environment.xml")

9. How do you access methods of .NET Objects?

We can create .Net objects and access their methods using DotNetFactory object.

The following example uses the CreateInstance method to create an instance of a blank Windows form object, display the form on screen, and then close it after two seconds.

```
Set formInstance = DotNetFactory.CreateInstance("System.Windows.Forms.Form", "System.Windows.Forms")

formInstance.Show

wait 2

formInstance.Close
```

10. How can you measure Time taken for script execution?

We can achieve this by using MercuryTimer Object. At the beginning of the program we can start execution by using MercuryTimer.Start and at the end we can stop timer by using MercuryTimer.Stop. Results file displays the time taken for program execution from Timer Start to Timer End.

11. How will you read Input and Output Parameters defined for Action using Programming?

This can be done by using Parameter object. For example if we define two Input Parameters UserName and Password we can read them as

```
Uname=Parameter("UserName")

Passwd=Parameter("Password")
```

12. How do you display a Random Number between 1 To 100?

```
randNum=RandomNumber(1,100)
```

CHAPTER 15

Descriptive Programming

1. What is a Descriptive Programming?

Descriptive Programming (DP) is a method of identifying an object using its properties directly with in the program statements.

2. In how many ways you can do descriptive programming?

There are two ways for writing code using descriptive programming.

- Using properties and values directly in the statement

The general syntax is:

```
TestObject("Prop1:= Value1","...",PropX:= ValueX")
```

- Using Description object

The general syntax is:

```
Set descObj=Description.create()
descObj("Prop1").value="Value1"
descObj("Prop2").value="Value2"
descObj("Prop3").value="Value3"
```

3. Out of above two ways which one is better?

First one is better if we want to identify a specific object using descriptive programming in only one or two lines.

Second one is better if we want to identify a specific object using descriptive programming in multiple lines. Second method is a clean coding approach and is easy to update property values based on changes in application values.

4. Write a Descriptive Programming Code to enter text into Google Edit box.

Using Description object we can set data in to Google Search edit box home page as

```
Set myDesc=Description.Create ()

myDesc("type").value="text"

myDesc("name").value="q"

myDesc("html tag").value="INPUT"

Browser("Google").Page("Google").WebEdit(myDesc).Set    "Cracking    QTP
Interviews"
```

5. Did you use descriptive programming in your project?

Yes. To identify the Runtime objects created in the application we have used descriptive programming.

6. What is a Run-Time object?

An object which is created in the application, based on the data we have used while script is running. For example if we order some products in ecommerce application a link will be created with the order number. Another example, if we create a lead in CRM application, a link will be created with the details of the lead.

Order link is created in the application based on the actions we performed and data we used in the script. Similarly lead link also. Hence Order link and Lead link in above examples are called Run Time Objects.

7. Give an example of how you work With RunTime Objects of an Application using Descriptive Programming

Members			
Login	First Name	Last Name	Level
admin	Administrator	Account	Administrator
guest	Guest	Account	Member
kiran	kiran	kumar	Member
sivareddy	SivaKoti	Reddy	Member
Insert			

Data Table

F9

	UserName	FirstName	LastName	Address	E
1	Kiran	Kiran	Kumar	Banglore	
2	SivaReddy	Siva	Reddy	Chennai	
3	Guest	Guest	QTP	NoIdea	
4					
5					
6					

```
Set usrLink=Description.Create()
usrLink("html tag").value="A"
For i=1 To Datatable.GetSheet("MemberUpdate").GetRowCount()
      usrLink("text").value=Datatable.GetSheet("MemberUpdate").
GetParameter("UserName").ValueByRow(i)
      Browser("Book Store").Page("Book Store").Link(usrLink).Click
            Browser("Book Store").Page("Book Store").Link(usrLink).Click
      Browser("Book   Store").Page("Book   Store").WebEdit("phone").Set
"12345678"
      Browser("Book  Store").Page("Book  store").  WebButton("Update").
Click
      wait(1)
Next
Set usrLink=Nothing
```

This program demonstrates how to use descriptive programming to deal with the RunTime objects created in the Application. RunTime object is the object created in the application while test script is under execution. Let us assume an automation requirement of registering 10 users and Updating their information by clicking on user name link. 10 users can be registered by having their data in Excel File. To update these users information we have to click on link object of each user and in a general approach these user link objects must present in repository. This is fine as long as usernames are known while creating the script. But in practical, these usernames are part of data file and are filled with new data every time before script execution. Hence we cannot have them in object repository while creating the script. The best and only solution to deal with this is Descriptive programming. The Above code reads usernames from data table during runtime and creates a user link object and clicks on the user link object.

Line 1-2: Creates Properties Collection object and sets html tag property as "**A**" representing the object as Link.

Line 3-4: Go through 1st to Last user name in excel file and reads username then assigns it to text property. If username read from excel file is Kiran object usrLink represent the link object Kiran.

Line5-6: Clicks the link represented by object usrLink

Line 7-8: Updates the information of the user represented by usrLink

8. Where else can you use descriptive programming?

- ➢ When we want to read child objects of a particular type from webPage. Below code will read all links from Google Home Page

```
set linkObjs=Browser("Google").Page("Home").ChildObject("html tag:=A")
```

- ➢ Objects in the application are dynamic in nature. For Example if you have to click on a link as "**Weather Report of Today 1/10/2010**" where the date is changing regularly to today's date we can use Descriptive programming as below.

```
Set weatherLink=Description.create()
weatherLink ("html tag").value="A"
weatherLink ("text").value= "Weather Report of Today "&Date()
Browser("App").Page("Admin").Link(weatherLink).click
```

- ➢ When we are automating applications having localization, instead of creating one object repository for each language we can use descriptive programming.

- Suppose if you want to start automation scripting much earlier to application availability.
- When Object repository size is getting huge.

9. Can we replace Object Repository with DP?

Ans: Even though it is possible; it is advised to use Object Repository. This is because it is easy to manage object property changes using Object Repository User Interface (UI).

10. What is a micClass?

Ans: micClass represents the class type of a test object like Browser, Page, WebList, WebButton.

11. Write a code to click on a link Advanced Search using DP?

Ans: Browser("IIBCEStore").Page("Home").Link("html tag:=A"," text:=Advanced Search"). click

12. Can you use variables in DP?

Ans: Yes. We can. Following code uses a variable ldata which stores the name of the link

```
ldata= "Advanced Search"

Browser("IIBCEStore").Page("Home").Link("html tag:=A", "text:="&ldata).
click
```

13. Write the code to click a link Advanced Search using Description Object?

Ans:

```
Set srchDesc=Description.Create ()

srchDesc ("text").value="Advanced Search"

srchDesc ("html tag").value="A"

Browser("IIBCEStore").Page("Home").Link(srchDesc).click
```

14. Write the code to print names of all links in a Page?

Ans:

```
Set linkDesc=Description.Create ()
```

```
linkDesc ("html tag").value="A"
Set chobjs=Browser("IIBCEStore").Page("Home").childObjects(linkDesc)
For i=0 To chobjs.count-1
      Print(chobjs(i).GetROproperty("text"))
Next
```

CHAPTER 16

Regular Expression

1. What is a Regular Expression?

A regular expression is a text string for describing pattern. We can think of regular expressions as another name to wildcard characters.

2. Where do you use Regular Expressions?

Regular Expressions can be used in:

(a) Defining Expected Results of Property values in Standard Check point

(b) Defining Physical Description of objects in the Repository

(c) Comparing Text Strings in Scripts

(d) Analysing Log files. Example: To find any lines in the log file starting with ERROR word

(e) For identifying Pop-Up Window based on its Title or Text using Regular Expression.

3. What Regular expression character * indicates?

* Matches the Previous character for Zero or more times.

Example:

```
iibc* => iib,iibc,iibcc,iibcccc
```

Note that in the previous example c is Previous Character to *. Hence it can be repeated for zero or more times.

4. How do you match alpha numeric characters in Regular Expression?

\w - Matches any alphanumeric characters including Underscore

5. How do you match Non-Digit characters in Regular Expression?

\D - Matches Non digit

6. How do you group Regular Expressions?

Multiple Regular Expression can be combined in to a Single Expression by using brackets ( )

Example:

```
Window("text:=.*(Report|Graph)").Close
```

The above line closes a Window with Text Report or Graph preceded by any set of alphanumeric characters.

7. How will you refer Regular Expression character as a normal character?

The backslash can be used along with a Regular Expression Character to indicate that the next character be treated as a literal character.

Example: If you want to check, the backslash can be used along with a Regular Expression Character to indicate that the next character be treated as a literal character.

Example: If you want to click a link with FirstName.LastName, script can be

```
Browser("Estore").Page("UserInfo").Link("text:=.*\..*").Click
```

Here the backslash is preceded by the .(period), so the .(period) will be considered as normal character & not as a Regular Expression.

8. How do you use Regular expression with VBScripting?

You can use regular expressions in VBScript by creating one or more instances of the RegExp object. This object allows you to find regular expression matches in strings, and replace regex matches in strings with other strings. You can create this object in scripting as **Regexp Rx= New Regexp**

9. Write Regular Expression for matching a blank line

^\s*$

The symbol ^ indicates from starting and $ indicates till ending. In other words ^ and $ at starting and Ending represents from starting to Ending of the string. \s indicates space i.e., blank data which is preceding character to *. Overall above expression represents space from starting to ending of the line i.e., the line is Blank.

10. Regular Expression to Check whether line starts with HARDWORK

^ HARDWORK

^ Symbol matches strings that are starting with specified pattern; In the above expression all strings starting with **HARDWORK** will be matched.

11. Regular Expression to Check whether line ends with SUCCESS

SUCCESS$

The **$** symbol matches strings that are ending with specified pattern, In the above expression all strings ending with SUCCESS will be matched.

12. How do you write Regular expression to represent a window whose title is today's date?

([0][1-9]|[1-2][0-9])|([3][0-1]) – ([0][1-9])|([1][0-2]) – ([1-9][0-9][0-9][0-9])

Description: Date is in the format DD-MM-YYYY where

DD- is Always between 01-31.

Whenever First D is 0 second D can be between 1-9; i.e 01-09; Hence Regular Expression [0][1-9]

If First D is 1-2 second D can be between 0-9; i.e 10-29; Hence Regular Expression [1-2][0-9]

If First D is 3 second D can be between 0-1; i.e 30-31; Hence Regular Expression [3][0-1]

Above Regular Expression for Day matches any day between 01-31

MM – is Always between 01-12

Whenever First M is 0 second M can be between 1-9; i.e 01-09; Representing January To September. Hence Regular Expression will be [0][1-9]

First M is 1 second M can be between 0-2; i.e 10-12; Representing October To December. Hence Regular Expression will be [1-2][0-9]

YYYY – is Between 1000 – 9999 with Regular Expression [1-9][0-9][0-9][0-9]

13. How do you write Regular expression to represent a window whose title is today's date?

([0][0-9])|([1][0-2]) : ([0-5][0-9]) : ([0-5][0-9]) (AM|PM)

Time will be in the format 10:25:46 AM where 10 represents Hours, 25 represents Minutes and 46 Represents Secs.

Since Hours are always between 00-12 regular expression is [0][0-9])|([1][0-2]). | specifies that hours are either 00-09 or 10-12

Since Minutes and Secs are always between 00-59 regular expression is [0-5][0-9])

Always Time Must show either AM or PM. Hence Regular Expression AM|PM represents either AM or PM.

14. Write a Regular Expression to match email address

(\w+)\.(\w+)@(\w+)\.[A-Za-z]{2,4}

Description: Matches any email ids in the format firstname.lastname@company.com

(\w+) – matches any Firstname with any Alphanumeric characters & Underscore

\. – treat dot as a literal character. Slash(\) is an escape character which escapes the special meaning of dot(.)

(\w+) – matches any lastname with any Alphanumeric characters & Underscore

@ - email id henceforth should be followed by @

(\w+)- matches any company name with any Alphanumeric characters & Underscore

\. – company name followed by a dot.

[A-Za-z]{2-4} – matches alphabets of both lower case and uppercase. Number of characters can range from two to four.

Matching Text: siva.reddy@i2brightcareers.com

sudhakar.k@i2brightcareers.com

Non-Matching Text: siva.reddy@ i2brightcareers.education

In the above expression string **education** exceeds the range 2-4 hence the expression does not match.

15. Write Regular Expression To match HTML Tag

<(.*)>.*<\/\1>

Description: The above expression Matches HTML Tags.

.* at starting Represents any Tag, and also since it is placed in (), it is the first positional data. 1 represents the end Tag must be the same as the 1st positional data. For example TABLE tag is stored in first positional data, 1 indicates that it must also have TABLE.* in between represents any text between two Tags.

Matching Text: <HEAD> Hello World </HEAD>

Non-Matching Text:

<HEAD> Hello World </IMG> : The initial tag is <HEAD> hence the end Tag must also be </HEAD> since the regular expression defines the end tag to be same as the first positional data.

16. Write a Program to display all lines starting with IIBC or iibc or IiBc in a text file?

Since string pattern should match IIBC, iibc, IiBc we have to consider string comparison as case insensitive. Code snippet is as follows....

```
Set fso=CreateObject("Scripting.FileSystemObject")

Set ts=fso.OpenAsTextStream ("D:\QTP\demolog.txt")

Set Rx=New RegExp

Rx. Pattern="^IIBC"

Rx.IgnoreCase=True

While NOT ts.AtEndOfStream

      l=ts.ReadLine()
```

```
    if Rx.Test(l) eqv True Then
          print(l)
    End If
Wend
```

17. Write a Program to replace word IIBC in a string with MYIIBC?

```
  Dim regEx, str1,str2 ,newStr              ' Create variables.
      str1 = "IIBC Good Morning."
      str2="MY IIBC"
  Set regEx = New RegExp              ' Create regular expression.
      regEx.Pattern = "IIBC"             ' Set pattern.
      regEx.IgnoreCase = True              ' Make case insensitive.
      newStr=regEx.Replace(str1, str2)    ' Make replacement.
print "String before Replace:"&str1
print "String after Replace:"&newStr
```

18. Write Regular Expression To match Credit Card Number

([4]{1})([0-9]{12,15})

Description: The above expression validates against a visa card number. Here all visa card numbers should start with a digit 4 and are followed by numbers ranging from 12 to 15 numbers.

Matching Text:

4125632152365, 4185632569852l4, 4125632569856321

Non-Matching Text:

3125652365214 : Here the first digit is not 4 hence the string is not matched.

41256321256 : Here first digit is 4 followed by 10 more numbers whereas the numbers following after 4 should be within the range of 12-15

42563985632156322 : The total numbers followed after first digit 4 is 16 which is out of the given range 12-15.

CHAPTER 17

Working with Data Table

1. What is the purpose of Data Table in QTP?

Data Table is used to store data used by QTP Scripts. Since we use various Testdata while scripts are executing we place all that data in Data table and read from there.

2. Why you should use various Test Data in the scripts?

Various sets of Test data helps to test the application more deeply by simulating the real world data used by various customers.

3. How many sheets Data Table contains?

Two types of sheets available

Global – Contains data shared by all the Actions

Local – Contains data which is specific to particular action.

By default one global and one action sheet is available. You can add as many sheets as you want through program.

4. How do you Program to read data from Datatable?

QTP has provided 3 objects to work with Data present in the Datatable. They are Data Table, DTSheet, DTParameter objects. These objects have many methods like AddSheet, AddParameter, Value, GetRowCount which will help us to program anything we require with datatable.

5. How can you read Help for Data Table Objects?

Two ways

- ➢ I can use help file. For example to find methods in DTSheet Object I have to do following

  QTP>Help>Quicktest Professional Help> HP QuickTest Professional Object Model Reference>Utility Objects>DTSheet
- ➢ Similarly to read help for DTParameter and DataTable objects

6. Write a code to add sheet Employees to the Data Table

Datatable.Addsheet "Employees"

7. How will you read number of rows in the Global Sheet?

Below specified lines are the various ways to read number of rows in the global sheet

```
rc1=Datatable.GetRowcount

rc2=Datatable.GetSheet("Global").GetRowCount

rc3=Datatable.GetSheet(dtGlobalSheet).GetRowCount

rc4=Datatable.GlobalSheet.GetRowCount
```

8. How do you know number of sheets present in the Data Table?

```
Datatable.GetSheetCount
```

9. Difference between import and importsheet methods?

import imports the entire excel file from an external location to QTP Datatable. importsheet will import specific sheet from an external location to QTP Datatable.

10. I have imported an excel file which has 10 sheets to Data table using import method. But I can see that only 3 sheets are imported. Why?

You might have only 2 actions in QTP that sums to 3 sheets in your datable. Since you have only 3 sheets in Data table import method can import only first 3 sheets.

11. What should I do if I want all 10 sheets to be imported?

You first need to add additional sheets to Data Table using AddSheet method. The number of sheets to be added is equivalent to 7 in this case since you already have 3 in the data table. Now try to import using import method, you should see all of them.

12. Difference between Export and Export Sheet Method

Export method exports entire data table to an external excel file. ExportSheet method exports specific sheet to an external excel file.

13. How will you export data table to an external excel file?

Below code exports Data table to an external excel file.

```
Datatable.export "D:\siva\data1.xls"
```

14. How will you export sheet from data table to external excel file?

This can be achieved by exportsheet method. Below code exports **Places** sheet from Data table to an external excel file *D:\siva\placesdata.xls*

```
Datatable.exportsheet "D:\siva\placesdata.xls","places"
```

15. How will you get the name of the current active sheet

```
Datatable.Localsheet.Name
```

```
Datatable.GetSheet(dtLocalSheet).Name
```

16. How will you get the name of the 3rd sheet?

```
Datatable.GetSheet (3).Name
```

17. How will you add a column to a Data Table?

Below code adds a parameter/column Asia and a country India to countries sheet

```
Datatable.GetSheet("countries").AddParameter "Asia","India"
```

18. I just want to add column, why this restriction of adding one compulsory value?

You are Right in your view. But have another view of why do you add a column without having even a single value in that. So QTP view is also right. Hence they made it mandatory.

19. What RawValue method of Parameter object will do?

If a cell contains Formula/Macro, RawValue method is used to read the formula. If we use Value or ValueByRow method they read the computed output of the formula.

20. How do you read a value from the cell of a data table?

I use **ValueByRow** method of a Parameter Object.

21. Do you have a method to read entire Row Data in a Data table?

No. We usually read data based on the column. If it is essential to read entire row I can write a function for the same.

22. What is the difference between Value, ValueByRow and RawValue methods?

Value, Value by Row reads the Value present in the cell and RawValue reads the macro present in the cell.

For example a cell B2 has a macro SUM(A1:D1)

Value, Value by Row returns the value present in B1 i.e the sum of the cells (A1 To D1) and **RawValue** returns a text string SUM(A1:D1) i.e the macro present in the cell.

If there is no Macro in the cell all works in same way.

23. How do you Get a sheet from Datatable?

We use **GetSheet** method to get the sheet object. Coding is as follows

```
set shobj=Datatable.Getsheet("sheetname")
```

Or

```
set shobj=Datatable.Getsheet(sheetID)
```

set is used since Getsheet method returns a sheet object.

24. Is statement Datatable ("EmpName") correct?

Yes it is correct. It Returns value present in the **EmpName** column of **Global Sheet** corresponding to the active row.

25. Is statement Datatable.Value ("EmpName") correct?

Yes it is correct. It Returns value present in the **EmpName** column of the **Global Sheet** corresponding to the active row.

26. What is the output of Datatable.Value("EmpName"," BangloreEmployees")

This will return the value present in the **EmpName** column of **BangloreEmployees** sheet corresponding to the active row.

27. Write a program to Read data from Excel sheet of excel file

```
Datatable.Addsheet "EmpInfo"
  Datatable.ImportSheet "C:\QTP\DataFiles\EmpData.xls","EmpInfo",
"EmpInfo"
set currentSheetObj=Datatable.GetSheet("EmpInfo")
set currentParamObj=currentSheetObj.GetParameter("Name")
rowCount=currentSheetObj.GetRowCount()
For row=1 To rowCount
           pmVal= currentParamObj.ValueByRow(row)
print(pmVal)
Next
```

28. How do you compare two cells in the Data table?

I can write a function like below which takes cell details as input and returns true or false depending on whether cells are having equal value or not.

s1,c1,r1 are sheet1 name, column and row values

s2,c2,r2 are sheet2 name, column and row values

Function CompareCells(s1,c1,r1,s2,c2,r2)

```
If  Datatable.GetSheet(s1).GetParameter(c1).ValueByRow(r1) = Datatable.
GetSheet(s2).GetParameter(c2).ValueByRow(r2)  Then
      CompareCells=True
Else
      CompareCells=False
End if
End Function
```

29. How do you delete column from Datatable?

We can use DeleteParameter method to delete the column

```
DataTable.GetSheet(dtGlobalSheet).DeleteParameter("ColumnName")
```

30. Can I load two excel files into Data table?

At a time Datatable can import data from one Excel File. If you import Data from another excel file it will replace existing data in the Datatable. However you can have a work around as follows.

Import first Excel File. Add additional sheets to the existing Data Table. Now import sheet by sheet from another excel file.

31. My Test Script to read data from an external Excel File is running without an error, but not able to see any data displaying. Why?

Most probable reason is Excel File might have been opened while Test Script is running. Please close that file and re-run the script. Mostly you can see data displaying.

CHAPTER 18

Scripting with Database

1. What is Database?

Database is used to store the data used by the application

2. We can use Text File to Store the Data. Why should we use Database?

Text File is not an efficient and secured way to store and retrieve large amount of data. So all enterprise applications uses Database to store and retrieve application data.

3. What is an SQL?

SQL is a structured query language which is used to retrieve the data from database

4. Where did you use database connectivity in your automation?

On various occasions we have to check the database. For example, when a user is registered whether his details are properly stored in the database, when we have updated user information is it being updated properly in the data base etc.

5. What are the Databases you have used in your automation?

I have developed scripts to retrieve data from different data bases depending on the application. Commonly I have used automation scripts for SQL Server and Oracle server databases to connect and retrieve data from databases.

6. My application uses MySQL database. In that case you don't have an experience of writing scripts to retrieve data from MySQL. How will you manage?

To work with any data base the connection string I use will vary. Other than that code will be more or less same. So I don't have any problem to write scripts for MYSQL server.

7. What following line will do?

```
Set db=CreateObject("ADODB.Connection")
```

Above code will creates an ADODB Connection object which is very essential to connect with Database. Above code is very commonly used code to write a script that works with database.

8. What is a connection string?

Connection string contains the information on how to connect to database. This information primarily contains Database Name, Data base driver to be used, Remote Server IP Address, User Name and Password.

9. I want to connect to MySQL server Database running on REMOTE Machine. What should I do?

First of all you must install MySQL Database Driver into your computer. You must also know Database Name, IP Address, User Name and Password to be used while interacting with data base.

10. How does the Connection string code for SQL Server look like?

Connection String looks like below for SQL Server

```
db.Open "Driver={SQL Server}; Server=iibcdbserver\mssql;
Database=edutracker; Uid=sa; Pwd=mypass;"
```

11. How will you connect to the database running on remote system?

If we provide the remote server Name/IPAddress in connection string I can connect to the remote Database and retrieve the Data.

12. How does the Connection string code for MySQL Server look like?

Connection String looks like below for MySQL Server

```
db.Open "Driver={MySQL ODBC 5.1 Driver}; Server=localhost; Database=prestashop; Uid=root; Pwd=mypass;"
```

13. What the following Code will do?

```
set rs = db.execute("SELECT * FROM ORDERS")
```

Above code will execute an SQL query on the connected database and returns the Record Set (rs). Execute is the method used to connect and execute a query on the databases.

14. Correct the errors in the following code

```
dbcon=CreateObject(ADODBConnection)

dbcon.execute "SELECT * FROM ORDERS"

db.Open "Driver={SQL Server}; Server=iibcdbserver\mssql; Database=edutracker; Uid=sa; Pwd=mypass;"
```

There are many errors in the above code

- ADODBConnection must be corrected as "ADODB.Connection ". Note dot(.) between ADODB and Connection.
- Dbcon is an object. So set is must
- Execute statement must be used after opening connection and returned result (recordset object) must be assigned to recordset object for further processing.
- Db.open must be changed to dbcon.open since data base connection object is assigned to dbcon.

Correct code is

```
set dbcon=CreateObject(ADODB.Connection)

dbcon.Open "Driver={SQL Server}; Server=iibcdbserver\mssql; Database=edutracker; Uid=sa; Pwd=mypass;"

set rs=dbcon.execute "SELECT * FROM ORDERS"
```

15. How can I read number of columns present in the Recordset?

Columns are also referred with Name Fields. Number of columns in a Recordset can be measured with following code syntax

```
colCount=rs.Fields.count
```

where rs represent Recordset.

Fields is a column collection

Count is used to get number of items(columns) in the Fields collection.

16. How do you read how many rows present in the RecordSet?

Number of rows in a Recordset can be measured by using RecordCount with following code syntax:

```
rowCount=rs.RecordCount
```

where rs represent Recordset.

RecordCount represent number of Records in the Record Set.

17. Why an EOF is used?

EOF means EndOfFile. Which is used to check whether we reached EndOfFile. Returns true if the current record position is after the last record, otherwise false

18. Is Following Code Correct?

```
While EOF

—

—

Wend
```

Ans: No. EOF must be used with rs object. So the correct syntax is

```
While rs.EOF

—

—

Wend
```

19. Can I read one entire row at a time from Recordset?

It is possible to read one or more rows at a time using GetRows method into a two dimensional array.

Following code syntax returns 3rd row into an array

```
arr=rs.GetRows(1,3)
```

20. What is the purpose of MoveNext?

MoveNext will move current record position to next record. There are other methods as shown below which are used to work with record positions.

Move - Moves the record pointer in a Recordset object

Syntax

```
Move(NoOfRecordsToMove,StartingPosition)
```

Startposition Values:

0 – Current

1 - First

2 - Last

MoveFirst - Moves the record pointer to the first record

MoveLast - Moves the record pointer to the last record

MoveNext - Moves the record pointer to the next record

MovePrevious -Moves the record pointer to the previous record

21. What the Following Code will do?

```
rs.MoveFirst
```

Above code moves Record position to starting

22. What the Following Code will do?

```
rs.MoveLast
```

Moves Record position to Last

23. What the Following Code will do?

```
rs.Move (3,1)
```

Above code moves Record position to 3rd from starting

24. What the Following Code will do?

```
rs.Move (3,1)

rs.Move (2,0)
```

The above code moves Record position to 6th from starting. First line moves record position to 3rd from starting and second line forwards/moves record position to an additional 2 more rows from current position.

25. What the Following code syntax will do?

```
rs.Move (3,1)

rs.Fields(3).value
```

Above code reads the value present in the 4th column and 3rd Row.

rs.Move (3,1) – Moved current record position to 3rd record/row

Fields (3) - Refers to 4th column because column index starts from 0

26. What the following code will do?

```
rs.fields(1).Name
```

Returns the name of the second column

27. What the following code will do?

```
For i=0 To rs.Fields.count-1

      Print(rs.fields(i).name)

Next
```

Above code prints the name of all columns present in the recordset.

Note: Above code print column names vertically as follows

```
EmpName

EmpPlace

EmpAge
```

If we want columns to be printed as row, code syntax must be slightly changed as follows

```
While rs.EOF
```

```
   header=""
For i=0 To rs.Fields.count-1
            header =rs.fields(i).name
            header = header &vbtab& celldata
Next
Print(header)
Wend
```

28. What the following code will do?

```
While rs.EOF
For i=0 To rs.Fields.count-1
            Print(rs.fields(i).value)
Next
Wend
```

The above code will go to infinite loop and will be keep printing the values present in all the columns of first row. This is because current record position has not been forwarded or moved to next row. To print values present in all columns of all rows we have to use the following code syntax:

```
While rs.EOF
For i=0 To rs.Fields.count-1
            Print(rs.fields(i).value)
Next
rs.MoveNext
Wend
```

Note: Above code doesn't print data row by row. For example if we have two rows as follows

```
Siva          IIBC       Testing
Anand         IIBC       DOT Net
```

Output of above code is

```
Siva
IIBC
Testing
Anand
IIBC
DOTNet
```

If we want data to be printed row by row code syntax must be slightly changed as follows:

While rs.EOF

```
   rowdata=""
For i=0 To rs.Fields.count-1
            celldata=rs.fields(i).value
            rowdata= rowdata&vbtab& celldata
Next
Print(rowdata)
rs.MoveNext
Wend
```

29. Write the code for following Activities.

A. Create Connection Object
B. Open connection to Database
C. Execute SQL query
D. Print all headers
E. Print all rows

Ans:

'Create Connection Object

```
Set db=CreateObject("ADODB.Connection")

'Open connection to Database

db.Open         "Driver={SQL     Server};     Server=iibcdbserver\mssql;
Database=edutracker; Uid=sa; Pwd=mypass;"

'Execute SQL query

set rs = db.execute("SELECT * FROM ORDERS")


'Print all headers

header=""

For i=0 To rs.Fields.count-1

            header =rs.fields(i).name

            header = header &vbtab& celldata

Next

Print(header)

'Print all rows

While rs.EOF

   rowdata=""

For i=0 To rs.Fields.count-1

            celldata=rs.fields(i).value

            rowdata= rowdata&vbtab&celldata

Next

Print(rowdata)

rs.MoveNext

Wend
```

CHAPTER 19

File System

1. What is a File System?

A file system is the core module in the operating system which is used to store and perform various operations on the files and Folders like Add,Delete,Copy and Edit etc.

2. What are the objects present in the VBScript FileSystem?

VBScript has following objects

- FileSystemObject
- Drive
- Folder
- File
- TextStream

3. What is TextStream object?

TextStream object refers to the data stream that is either coming out of file or going into file. We will get TextStream object when we open the file for reading or writing.

4. While Reading from File how do you know you have reached End of File?

Reaching End of File can be found by using **AtEndOfStream** property of TextStream Object. If End of File is Reached AtEndOfStream will return True, else it will return False.

In other words if still data is there to read AtEndOfStream will return False. This means If it returns False we must read from file. Code syntax will be as follows:

```
While NOT ts.AtEndOfStream

—

—

Wend
```

5. Does blank line in a text File is considered as End of Stream?

Ans: No. Blank Lines and Spaces are part of file like any other characters. So they are not treated as End of Stream

6. Write a program to read data from a text file?

```
Const ForReading = 1

Dim fso, ts

Set fso = CreateObject("Scripting.FileSystemObject")

Set ts = fso.OpenTextFile ("c:\logfile.txt", ForReading)

While not ts.AtEndOfStream

      print(ts.ReadLine())

Wend

Set fso=nothing

Set ts =nothing
```

7. Write a program to write data into a text file

```
Const ForWriting = 2

Dim fso, ts

Set fso = CreateObject ("Scripting.FileSystemObject")

Set ts = fso.OpenTextFile ("c:\testfile.txt", ForWriting,true)

For i=1 To 100

      ts.WriteLine("Hello World")
```

```
Next
Set fso=nothing
Set ts=nothing
```

8. What is Collection?

Collection is nothing but group of objects.

9. How do you find number of objects in a collection?

Collection has count method. Using this we can find how many objects are there in the collection.

10. What Collections are available in File System?

There are 3 collections available

- Drives
- Folders
- Files

11. How will you read the Name of the File or Folder?

File and Folder Objects are having **Name** property which can be used to read the name of the File or Folder any time.

12. How do you check whether file Exists or Not?

```
Set fso = CreateObject("Scripting.FileSystemObject")
If (fso.FileExists("D:\IIBC\mydata.txt")) Then
   msg = "file exists."
Else
   msg = "file doesn't exist."
End If
```

13. How will you rename a File?

```
Set fso = CreateObject("Scripting.FileSystemObject")
fso.MoveFile "D:\QTP\mydata.txt", " D:\QTP\mydata_new.txt"
```

14. Write a program to rename a folder

```
Dim fso, fdr

Set fso = CreateObject("Scripting.FileSystemObject")

Set fdr = fso.GetFolder("C:\folderA")

fdr.Name="folderB"
```

15. Write a program to display all subfolders in a given folder tree

```
Function GetSubFolders(fdrPath)

Dim fso, fd

   Set fso = CreateObject("Scripting.FileSystemObject")

   Set fd=fso.GetFolder(fdrPath)

   Set fc = fd.subfolders 'fc - folder collection

    For each fdr in fc

      subfdr= fdrPath &"\"&fdr.name

      print (subfdr)

      GetSubFolders (subfdr)

     Next

End Function

GetSubFolders ("D:\QTP")
```

16. What is a Dictionary Object?

Dictionary object is used to store key value pair. For example if we want to store Karnataka – Bangalore, TamilNadu – Chennai, Kerala – Trivandrum we can use dictionary object.

17. Write a program to print all drives in the file system

```
Dim fso, d, dc

Set fso = CreateObject("Scripting.FileSystemObject")

Set dc = fso.Drives
```

```
For Each d in dc

     print(d.DriveLetter)

Next
```

18. Write a program to print the free space in a given drive

```
Dim fso, d, s

drv="C:\"

Set fso = CreateObject("Scripting.FileSystemObject")

Set d = fso.GetDrive(fso.GetDriveName(drv))

s = "Drive " & d. driveletter & vbTab

s = "Drive " & d. driveletter & " has Free Space: " & FormatNumber(d.
FreeSpace/1024, 0)  & " Kbytes"

Msgbox(s)
```

CHAPTER 20

Working with XML

1. What is an XML?

XML or Extensible Markup Language is a markup language that you can use to create your own tags.

2. Is XML next version of HTML?

No. XML is not a replacement for HTML and they were designed with different goals. HTML was designed to display data and to focus on how data looks and XML was designed to describe data and to focus on what data is. HTML is about displaying information, XML is about describing information.

3. How an XML file Looks Like?

```
<address>
  <name "Author=Siva", "Place=IIBC">
    <title>Mrs.</title>
    <first-name> Mary </first-name>
    <last-name> McGoon </last-name>
  </name>
  <street>
    1401 Main Street
  </street>
  <city>Any town</city>
</address>
```

4. What an XML file contains?

There are three common terms used to describe parts of an XML document: *tags*, *elements*, and *attributes*.

- A tag is the text between the left angle bracket (<) and the right angle bracket (>).
  Example: Starting tags: <name>,<title>

  Ending tags: </name>,</title>

- An element is the starting tag, the ending tag, and everything in between. In the sample above, the <name> element contains three child elements: <title>, <first-name>, and <last-name>.
- An attribute is a name-value pair inside the starting tag of an element. Author and Place are attributes, Siva and IIBC are values respectively.

5. How is XML used in Projects?

XML is used in many aspects of web development as follows.

Data Sharing

XML data is stored in plain text format. So XML data can easily be exchanged between incompatible systems and different applications

Data Separation

If you need to display dynamic data in your HTML document, data can be stored in separate XML files. With a few lines of JavaScript, you can read an external XML file and update the data content of your HTML without need for any changes to the HTML.

Enhanced Data Availability

Since XML is independent of hardware, software and application, XML can make your data more available and useful. With XML, your data can be available to all kinds of "reading machines" like Handheld computers, voice machines, news feeds, etc.

Creating New Internet Languages

A lot of new Internet languages are created with XML.

- XHTML the latest version of HTML
- WSDL for describing available web services
- WAP and WML as markup languages for handheld devices
- RSS languages for news feeds
- RDF and OWL for describing resources and ontology
- SMIL for describing multimedia for the web

6. What is DTD?

Document Type Definition or **DTD** defines the elements that can appear in an XML document, the order in which they can appear, how they can be nested inside each other.

7. What is XML Schema?

Schema is also like DTD except that it can also define data types and more complicated rules than a DTD can.

8. How will you read Root Element Name in an XML file?

```
Set xd = XMLUtil.CreateXMLFromFile("D:\QTP\GlobalConfig.xml")
set rootElement= xd.GetRootElement()
rootElementName = rootElement.ElementName
Msgbox(rootElementName)
```

9. How will you read attributes of a Root Element?

```
Set xd = XMLUtil.CreateXMLFromFile("D:\QTP\GlobalConfig.xml")
set rootElement = xd.GetRootElement
set attrCol= rootElement.Attributes
For i=1 To attrCol.count
     Set attr=attrCol.Item(i)
     print(attr.name&"="&attr.value)
Next
```

10. How will you compare Two XML files?

```
Set xml1 = XMLUtil.CreateXMLFromFile("D:\QTP\Config1.xml")
Set xml2 = XMLUtil.CreateXMLFromFile("D:\QTP\ Config2.xml")
res= xml1.Compare(xml2,diffResult)
If res  eqv True  Then
      Msgbox ("TwoXML files are Same")
Else
      Msgbox("Two XML files are different")
End If
```

CHAPTER 21

Automation Object Model (AOM) and Document Object Model (DOM)

AUTOMATION OBJECT MODEL (AOM)

1. What is an Object Model?

An Object model is a collection of classes or objects which can be controlled or studied by any program. An Object Model gives a facility to control the functionality of an application programmatically.

2. What is QTP Automation Object Model?

The Quick Test Automation Object Model is a set of its classes and interfaces, together with their properties, methods and events, and their relationships. All configuration and run functionality provided via the QuickTest interface is in some way represented in its Object Model.

3. When is AOM used?

Initialization scripts: These scripts automatically start QuickTest and configure the options and the settings required for testing a specific environment.

Updating values: This includes updating the tests with the proper add-ins, runs it in update run mode against an updated application, and saves it.

Applying new options to existing tests: When a test needs to be updated with a new version of QuickTest, and if that newer version offers a new option that needs to be updated in all existing scripts.

Calling QuickTest from other applications: Sometimes a simple web/windows application may be required to schedule the test runs. This is useful for non technical people.

Some more situations where QuickTest Automation Programs are required

- ➢ To configure multiple tests with same settings
- ➢ To configure QTP for different environments/machines
- ➢ For passing test parameter values from one test to another
- ➢ To define environment variables
- ➢ When there are preconditions to execute before actual test execution
- ➢ To configure the test object identification properties

4. What is the difference between AOM Scripts and QTP Scripts?

QTP Scripts are developed to Test the Application/Project. But the AOM scripts are developed to operate QTP. For example, using QTP we can run only one test at a time. If we want to run multiple tests, we have to go for Test Batch Runner. But using AOM we can automate QTP functionality. We can write a script in AOM to open a Test, execute, store the result and again do the same with another test.

5. Where do you execute AOM Scripts?

AOM doesn't meant use in QTP. But it is developed to access QTP from various places. For example, we can run QTP scripts from Quality Center. This is happening because the QC is having inbuilt AOM API's to access QTP by using its object model. Like the same way we can develop a tool to control QTP operations. So in these scenarios the AOM scripts will be executed in QC or in the Developed Tool.

6. How do you access AOM in QTP?

Not only in QTP, we can access AOM in any place by using below statement.

```
Set qtApp = CreateObject("QuickTest.Application")
```

Here createobject is a vbscript inbuilt function to access Automation Object. "QuickTest. Application" is a class developed to access QTP.

7. In which language do you write AOM Scripts?

QTP AOM is an Object Model. It can be accessed by using any language. But when accessing AOM in QTP you must use VBScript because QTP support only VBScript.

Below are some examples for creating the QuickTest Application object and starting QuickTest in visible mode, using different programming languages.

Visual Basic

```
1.    Dim qtApp As QuickTest.Application
2.    Set qtApp = New QuickTest.Application
3.    qtApp.Launch
4.    qtApp.Visible = True
```

The example below can be used only after setting a reference to the type library. If you are not working in a development environment that allows referencing type libraries create the Application object as described for VBScript below.

Code Walkthrough

Line1: Declare qtApp as an application object

Line2: Create and assign Application object to qtApp

Line3: Start QuickTest

Line4: Make it visible

VBScript

```
1.    Dim qtApp
2.
3.    Set qtApp = CreateObject("QuickTest.Application")
4.    qtApp.Launch
5.    qtApp.Visible = True
```

Code Walkthrough

Line1: Declare qtApp

Line3: Create and assign Application object to qtApp

Line4: Start QuickTest

Line5: Make it visible

```
1.    var qtApp = new ActiveXObject("QuickTest.Application");
2.    qtApp.Launch();
3.    qtApp.Visible = true
```

JavaScript

Code Walkthrough

Line1: Declare, Create and assign Application object to qtApp

Line2: Start QuickTest

Line3: Make it visible

Visual C++

```
1.    #import "QTObjectModel.dll"
2.    QuickTest::_ApplicationPtr spApp;
3.    spApp.CreateInstance("QuickTest.Application");
4.    spApp->Launch();
5.    spApp->Visible = VARIANT_TRUE;
```

Code Walkthrough

Line1: Import the type library

Line2: Declare the application pointer and assign to spApp

Line3: Create Application object to spApp

Line4: Start QuickTest

Line5: Make it visible

8. How do you run Multiple Tests without using Test Batch Runner?

The below script execute 10 tests with name Test1,Test2....Test10 which are there in the same folder.

```
' Declare the Application object variable
Dim qtApp
' Declare a Test object variable
Dim qtTest
```

```
‘ Declare a Run Results Options object variable
Dim qtResultsOpt

‘ Create the Application object
Set qtApp = CreateObject(“QuickTest.Application”)
‘ Start QuickTest
qtApp.Launch

‘ Make the QuickTest application visible
qtApp.Visible = True

For iTestIndex=1 to 10

 ’ Open the test in read-only mode
 qtApp.Open ”C:\Tests\Test”&iTestIndex, True

 ’ set run settings for the test
 Set qtTest = qtApp.Test

 ’ Create the Run Results Options object
 Set qtResultsOpt = CreateObject(“QuickTest.RunResultsOptions”)
 ’ Set the results location
qtResultsOpt.ResultsLocation = ”C:\Tests\Test”&iTestIndex&”\Res1”

 ’ Run the test with specified result foder
 qtTest.Run qtResultsOpt

 ’ Close the test
 qtTest.Close

Next

‘Release Variables
Set qtResultsOpt = Nothing
Set qtTest = Nothing
Set qtApp = Nothing
```

9. How do you run scripts in remote machine?

By default you can be able to execute QTP scripts on a Local Machine. Automation Object Model is providing a facility to execute QTP scripts on a Remote Machine.

When you use **CreateObject("QuickTest.Application")**, it is giving permissions to execute scripts in local machine's QTP.

To execute scripts in Remote Machine use

```
Set qtApp = CreateObject("QuickTest.Application", "Remote Machine Name")
```

Before using this statement ensure that the Distributed COM (DCOM) Configuration Properties of the remote computer are set to allow you to run QuickTest Professional Automation from your computer.

Steps to Set the DCOM Configuration Properties on Remote Machine

- On the computer where you want to run the automation script, choose Start—> Run. The Run dialog box opens.
- Enter **DCOMCNFG** and click OK. The Distributed COM Configuration Properties dialog box or the Component Services window opens (depending on your operating system) and displays the list of COM applications available on the computer.
- Select QuickTest Professional Automation from the list and open the Properties dialog box for the application. (Click the Properties button or right-click and choose Properties, depending on your operating system.)
- In the QuickTest Professional Automation Properties dialog box, click the Security tab.
- In the launch permissions section, choose the custom option and click Edit.
- Use the **Add** and **Remove** options to select the network users or groups for which you want to allow or deny permission to launch QuickTest Professional via an automation script. When you are finished, click **OK** to save your settings.
- Repeat steps 5 and 6 for the configuration permissions section to select the users or groups who can modify QuickTest Professional configuration options via an automation script.
- In the QuickTest Professional Automation Properties dialog box, click the **Identity** tab and select the **interactive user** option.
- Click **OK** to save the QuickTest Professional Automation Properties settings.
- Click **OK** to close the Distributed COM Configuration Properties dialog box or the Component Services window.

10. How do you hide QTP when running?

```
' Create the Application object
Set qtApp = CreateObject(“QuickTest.Application”)

' Make the QuickTest application Invisible
qtApp.Visible = False
```

11. How do you know the version of QTP?

We can know the version in two ways

By using Environment Values

```
Msgbox Environment(“ProductVer”)
```

By using AOM

```
Set qtp=CreateObject(“quicktest.application”)

msgbox qtp.Version
```

12. How do you know that QTP is maximized / minimized?

```
Set qtp=CreateObject(“quicktest.application”)

msgbox qtp.WindowState
```

13. What is the limitation of using AOM in QTP?

When you access AOM in QTP, we can't change the settings of QTP. But we can know what settings are configured.

14. How do you Pause, Continue and Stop the Test Run?

```
' Declare the Application object variable
Dim qtApp
' Declare a Test object variable
Dim qtTest
' Declare a Run Results Options object variable
Dim qtResultsOpt

' Create the Application object
Set qtApp = CreateObject(“QuickTest.Application”)
```

```
' Start QuickTest
qtApp.Launch

' Make the QuickTest application visible
qtApp.Visible = True

' Open the test in read-only mode
qtApp.Open "C:\Tests\Test1", True

' set run settings for the test
Set qtTest = qtApp.Test

' Create the Run Results Options object
Set qtResultsOpt = CreateObject("QuickTest.RunResultsOptions")

' Set the results location
qtResultsOpt.ResultsLocation = "C:\Tests\Test1\Res1"

' Run the test with specified result foder
qtTest.Run qtResultsOpt

'Pause the Test Run
qtTest.Pause

'Continue the Test run
qtTest.Continue

'Stop the Test run
qtTest.Stop

' Close the test
qtTest.Close

'Release Variables
Set qtResultsOpt = Nothing
Set qtTest = Nothing
Set qtApp = Nothing
```

15. How can you run the tests in update run mode?

```
' Declare the Application object variable
Dim qtApp
' Declare a Test object variable
Dim qtTest
' Declare a Run Results Options object variable
Dim qtResultsOpt
' Declare a Update Run Object Options object variable
Dim qtUpdateRunOptions

' Create the Application object
Set qtApp = CreateObject("QuickTest.Application")
' Start QuickTest
qtApp.Launch

' Make the QuickTest application visible
qtApp.Visible = True

 ' Open the test in read-only mode
 qtApp.Open "C:\Tests\Test1", True

 ' set run settings for the test
 Set qtTest = qtApp.Test

 ' Create the Run Results Options object
 Set qtResultsOpt = CreateObject("QuickTest.RunResultsOptions")

 ' Set the results location
 qtResultsOpt.ResultsLocation = "C:\Tests\Test1\Res1"

' Prepare the UpdateRunOptions object
Set qtUpdateRunOptions = CreateObject("QuickTest.UpdateRunOptions")
' Update the Active Screen
qtUpdateRunOptions.UpdateActiveScreen = True

'Update Test object descriptions
qtUpdateRunOptions.UpdateCheckpoints = True

```

```
'Update checkpoint values
qtUpdateRunOptions.UpdateTestObjectDescriptions = True

' Run the test in Update Run mode
qtApp.Test.UpdateRun qtUpdateRunOptions, qtRunResultsOptions

' Save the test
qtApp.Test.Save

 ' Close the test
 qtTest.Close

'Release Variables
Set qtUpdateRunOptions = Nothing
Set qtResultsOpt = Nothing
Set qtTest = Nothing
Set qtApp = Nothing
```

16. How do you find in which version of QTP the test was developed?

```
Set qtp=CreateObject("quicktest.application")

msgbox qtp.CreatedinVersion
```

17. How do you get Action names of a test?

```
'Declare the Application object variable
Dim qtApp

' Create the Application object
Set qtApp = CreateObject("QuickTest.Application")

'Get Actions Count
TotalActionCount=qtApp.Test.Actions.Count

'Get Action Names by index
For aIndex=1 to TotalActionCount
 msgbox qtApp.Test.Actions.Item(aIndex).Name
Next

```

```
' Release the Application object
Set qtApp = Nothing
```

18. How do you set the specific panes to be visible in QTP?

```
'Declare the Application object variable
Dim qtApp

' Create the Application object
Set qtApp = CreateObject("QuickTest.Application")

' Start QuickTest
qtApp.Launch

' Display the Expert View
qtApp.ActivateView "ExpertView"

' Display the Active Screen pane
qtApp.ShowPaneScreen "ActiveScreen", True

' Hide the Data Table pane
qtApp.ShowPaneScreen "DataTable", False

' Display the Debug Viewer pane
qtApp.ShowPaneScreen "DebugViewer", True

' Maximize the QuickTest window
qtApp.WindowState = "Maximized"

' Make the QuickTest window visible
qtApp.Visible = True

' Release the Application object
Set qtApp = Nothing
```

DOCUMENT OBJECT MODEL INTERVIEW QUESTIONS

1. What is Document Object Model?

The Document Object Model (DOM) is an application programming interface (API) developed by the World Wide Web Consortium (W3C) to create and modify HTML pages and XML documents. It defines the logical structure of documents in the way a document is accessed and manipulated.

With the Document Object Model, programmers can create and build documents, navigate their structure and add, modify, or delete elements and content. Anything found in an HTML or XML document can be accessed, changed, deleted, or added using the Document Object Model. The Document Object Model can be used with any programming or scripting languages.

2. When to use DOM?

An object in a HTML document will have lot of properties and supported methods. But QTP captures only limited properties that are useful to find the object. All native methods and properties of a html object cannot be captured or performed directly by QTP. DOM is especially useful for identifying Parent Nodes, Previous and Next Elements.

3. When should we not use DOM in QTP?

Not for Browser Compatibility Testing
In QTP, DOM methods and properties can work only for Internet Explorer. So if the application needs to be tested in different browsers then the DOM should not used in the scripts because it may affect the result.

Note: QTP 11 support DOM for Firefox.

Not for FireEvents
QTP performs DOM operations on application in offline mode. i.e. when performing DOM operations QTP will not activate the browser. In this case fire events will not work properly.

Not for Edit box, Combo box Validations
The edit and combo boxes accept any value which is coming from DOM methods. Even if the objects are disabled or restricted to use specific characters.

4. How do you access DOM methods/properties for an object?

In QTP, for every web object there is a property called "object". Using this property the internal methods and properties can be accessed for any web object.

Syntax:

```
WebObjectClass("").Object
```

WebObjectClass: - Any test object class related to web

Object: - A property to access internal methods and properties of a web object

Ex: The below script will get Ready state of the browser

```
Browser("browser").Object.ReadyState
```

5. What is Document object?

Document object is the root object in DOM. To do any operations on a HTML document, first we have to get the document object.

6. What is the difference between browser and document object?

A browser is the one which understands a server side technology and display as html page. A document object is the html document which can be stored in any browser. We can navigate between html pages using browser object.

7. How do we use native properties in Object Repository for an object?

We can configure a new property as an identification property in Object Identification window. To configure that

Go to Tools → Object Identification window → Select Web Environment → Under Mandatory properties list Click on Add/Remove

A new window opens which a list of properties has specified.

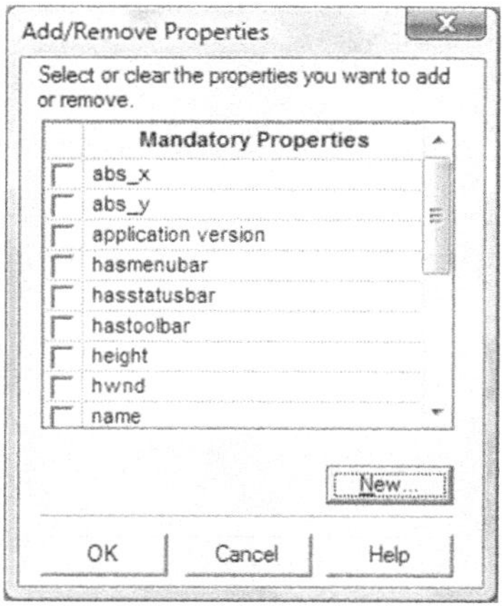

Any defined property will get added in this list. To define a property click on new. New Property dialog opens.

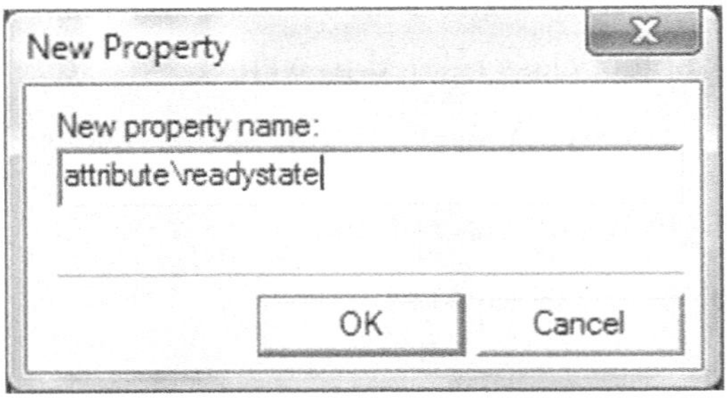

In the above dialog enter "Attribute/property name". Automatically whenever an object is added from that class, the object will have the configured property with value. When you spy on the object, the property will be displayed in Identification Properties list.

8. How do you focus on an object?

Focus is a native method which will be used to focus on an object.

Ex: Browser("Gmail").Page("Gmail").WebEdit("Email").Object.focus

9. How do you get the parent element of an object?

```
Set lnkObj= Browser("Gmail").Page("Gmail").Link("Learn more")

Msgbox lnkObj.Object.parentElement.outerHTML
```

10. How do you identify the next object of an object?

```
set    obj=Browser("Gmail").Page("Gmail").Link("Learn    more").Object.
previousSibling

 msgbox obj.outerhtml
```

11. How do you identify the previous object of an object?

```
set    obj=Browser("Gmail").Page("Gmail").Link("Learn    more").Object.
NextSibling

 msgbox obj.outerhtml
```

CHAPTER 22

QTP and QC

1. What is the pre-requisite to run the QTP scripts in QC?

- QTP Connectivity Add-In and QTP Add-ins are installed
- Check Allow other Mercury products to run tests and components present under Tools > Options > Run in QTP

2. How to connect QTP from QC test plan?

Using Launch button in the Test Script tab under test plan module

3. From which QC modules can QTP be launched?

- Test Plan (Launch button in the Test Script tab)
- Test Lab (Run Automation script in the test lab)

4. How to connect QC from QTP?

- Go to File -> Quality Center Connection.
- Enter QC URL and click Connect.
- Log in with valid user credentials.
- Select the Domain and Project

5. Write a script to launch the QTP and connect to QC

```
Set qtqcApp = CreateObject("QuickTest.Application")

qtqcApp.Launch 'Launch QTP

qtqcApp.Visible = True 'Make it visible

'Connect to Quality Center

qtqcApp.TDConnection.Connect "QC URL",

"Domain", "Project", "user id", "password", False
```

6. Can the test set contain manual and automation scripts?

Yes

7. Which object would be used to access QC OTA (Open Test Architecture) objects in QTP script?

QCUtil

8. Write a script to check the QC is connected or not and report the server, domain and project names if connected?

```
if QCUtil.IsConnected then

    Reporter.ReportEvent 0, "Connected", "Connected to server: " + QCUtil.TDConnection.ServerName + chr (13) +"Project: " + QCUtil.TDConnection.ProjectName + chr (13) + "Domain: " + QCUtil.TDConnection.DomainName

else

    Reporter.ReportEvent 1, "Not connected", "Not connected to Quality Center"

end if
```

9. Write a script to report the defect in QC with status, summary and detected by fields.

```
Dim QCCon

Set QCCon = QCUtil.TDConnection

Set BugFactory = QCCon.BugFactory
```

```
Set Bug = BugFactory.AddItem (Nothing)

Bug.Status = "New"

Bug.Summary = "New defect"

Bug.DetectedBy = "admin" ' user that must exist in the database's user
list

Bug.Post
```

10. Write a script to display the current test set name?

```
Set CurrentTSTest = QCUtil.CurrentTestSet

Reporter.ReportEvent 2,"Current TestSet", CurrentTSTest.Name
```

11. What is the TDConnection?

- It is a property of QCUtil object
- It represents the current QC session and provides the access to QC object model

12. Is there version control in QC with QTP?

Yes, QTP 10.0 provides you the version control feature under the name of Quality Center Version Control present under File Menu. Earlier versions of QTP can work with 3rd party version control tools

13. Write a script to attach the file to QC current test run?

```
Set obj_Afact = QCUtil.Currentrun.Attachments

Set obj_Att = obj_Afact.AddItem(Null)

obj_Att.FileName = FileName

obj_Att.Type = 1

obj_Att.Post
```

14. Write a script to add a file to 'Subject\Automation' folder attachments in the test plan?

```
qcfp = "Subject\Automation"

Set otaTreeManager = QCUtil.TDConnection.TreeManager
```

```
Set otaSysTreeNode = otaTreeManager.NodeByPath(qcfp)

Set otaAttachmentFactory = otaSysTreeNode.Attachments

Set obj_Att = otaAttachmentFactory(Null)

obj_Att.FileName = FileName

obj_Att.Type = 1

obj_Att.Post
```

15. Write a script to get the attached file from Subject\Automation folder in QC test plan?

```
qcfp = "Subject\Automation"

FileName = "TestData.xls"

Set otaTreeManager = QCUtil.TDConnection.TreeManager

Set otaSysTreeNode = otaTreeManager.NodeByPath(qcfp)

Set otaAttachmentFactory = otaSysTreeNode.Attachments

Set otaAttachmentFilter = otaAttachmentFactory.Filter

 intNdId = otaSysTreeNode.NodeID

otaAttachmentFilter.Filter("CR_REFERENCE") = "'ALL_LISTS_" & intNdId &
"_" & FileName & "'"

Set otaAttachmentList = otaAttachmentFilter.NewList

If otaAttachmentList.Count > 0 Then

     Set otaAttachment = otaAttachmentList.Item(1)

     otaAttachment.Load True," "

     fPath = otaAttachment.FileName

Else

     Reporter.reportevent 1,"Get Attachment: ","File is not found"

End If
```

16. Can we record Quality Center operations with QTP?

Yes, only with QC 9.2 and above. Use .NET Add-in

17. Can we schedule a test run from Quality Center?

Yes, use 'Test Run Scheduler' utility that comes with QC

18. How can you run only selected scripts instead of running the whole test set?

- Select the scripts you want to execute in the test set
- Click Run button

19. What is Business Process Testing in QC?

Each scenario that the Subject Matter Expert creates is a business process test. A business process test is composed of a serial flow of components. Each component performs a specific task. A component can pass data to a subsequent component.

20. Can you use BPT framework without QC?

- No, It is built-in Automation Framework in QC
- It requires a separate license to use BPT

21. Where can you create the Component?

Components can be created in QC or QTP with QC connected

22. What are the different types of components?

- Two types of components
- Scripted Component: created using VBScript
- Business Component: created using Keyword driven script

23. Where can you create a component in QC?

In Business Components Module

24. Where can you create Business Process Test in QC?

In the Test Plan module

25. Is it possible to copy the scripts from one project to another?

Yes, Scripts can be copied in to different QC project

26. Is it possible to copy the attachments in the test plan ex: repositories and lib files in to another project?

YES, copy the entire folder

27. How to create Script Template for Manual Test Case in QC?

- Create Manual test case under the folder in Subject
- Design the test steps and click Generate button in Design steps tab
- select script type as QTP Script
- Go to Test Script tab, you can see the script template generated for the test case

28. Tell me all the modules available in QC.

- Releases
- Requirements
- Test Plan
- Test Lab
- Defects
- Business Components

29. Can we do spell and grammar checks in QC?

YES, available under Tools

30. How can you change the Project in QC?

Using Change Project option under Tools

31. How can you copy the QTP script from the local machine to "Subject\Automation" folder in QC?

1. In QTP Open; **File - > Quality Center Connection**
2. Enter QC url
3. Click Connect button, QC would be connected
4. Enter QC UserID and Password and click Authenticate button
5. Select Domain & Project and click Login button

6. Open the script in QTP you wish to save, click on File - > Save As option
7. Select Quality Center button in the corner of the Save dialog
8. Select the relevant subject folder in QC
9. Click on OK

32. How can you copy the QTP script from the local machine to "Root\Automation" folder in QC?

It is not possible to save the script in QC Test Lab, so script can't be copied/saved to "Root\Automation" folder in QC

33. How to convert manual test case in to Automation Test Case in QC?

1. In Test Plan module select your desired manual test.
2. Click on the Design Steps Tab and verify test is correct test.
3. Click on the Generate Script button and select 'QUICKTEST_TEST'
4. The manual test will be converted to an automated test and the test script tab will have a pre-generated script with only report steps for each of the design steps of the manual test.
5. Click on the "Launch Quick Test Pro" button to edit the script in QTP with the actual script.

34. How to add snapshot of the application to QC?

1. Click Snapshot button in the Attachments tab
2. Drag the Camera icon from the Snapshot dialog onto an object that you want to capture
3. Snapshot would be displayed in the snapshot dialog
4. Click Attach button

35. I could not see the Launch QTP button in the Test Script tab for QTP script in the Test Plan. What could be the reason?

Check the QTP Add-in is installed properly

36. Can we run the scripts at specific date and time on specific remote machines from QC?

Yes, we can schedule the test run for specific date & time on specific machine in the network

37. How can you schedule the test run in QC?

Test scripts can be scheduled using Execution and Time dependent conditions in the Test Lab

38. Where can you define the Execution and Time dependent conditions for the test set?

Execution and Time dependent conditions can be defined for the tests in Execution Flow Tab under Test Lab module

39. QuickTest_Test Type option is not available in Automation test type list after clicking Generate Script button. What is the reason?

QTP add-in is not installed

40. What is the System Test in QC?

Using system tests, you can instruct Quality Center to provide system information for a machine, capture a desktop image, or restart a machine.

41. How to create a System Test in QC?

1. Choose a subject folder in the test plan tree.
2. Click the New Test button, or choose Tests > New Test. Create New Test dialog box opens

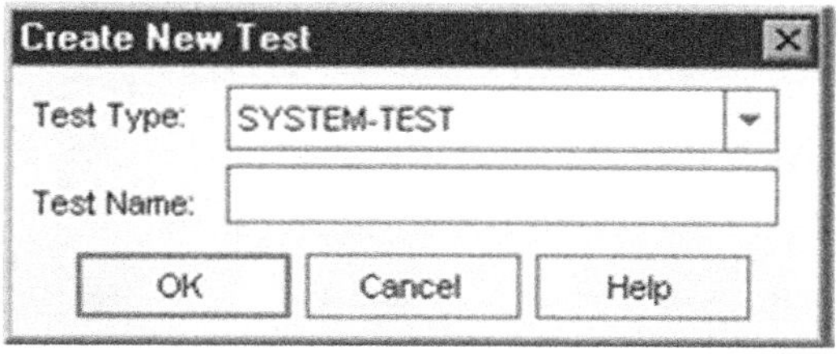

3. In the Test Type list box, select SYSTEM-TEST
4. Enter test name and click OK button
5. Select System Test created in the Test Plan and click on Test Script Tab

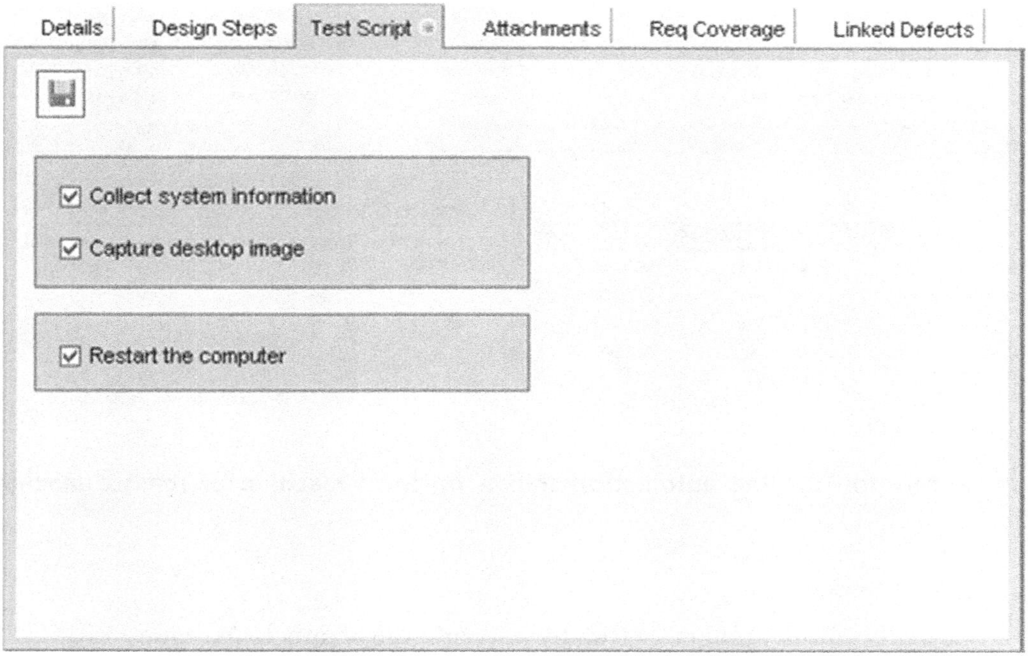

6. Select System Test options
7. Click Save button

42. What is the pre-requisite to run System Test?

To run a system test, you must install the System Test Remote Agent Add-in and the HP Quality Center Connectivity Add-in on the machine where the test is to be run.

43. What is the tab name where we can run the test sets in the Test Lab?

Execution Grid

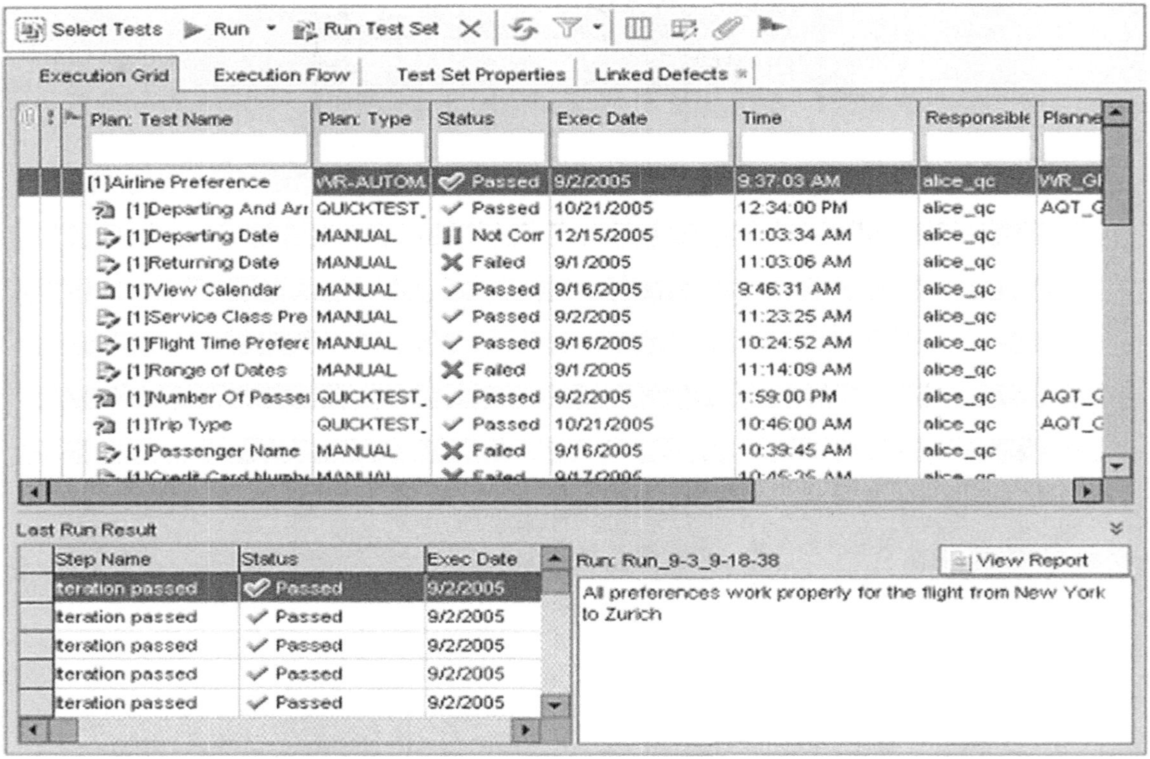

44. How can you run the automation scripts on local machine or remote machines in QC?

1. Select Test Set
2. Click either Run Test Set or Run by selecting the scripts to execute
3. Automatic Test Runner dialog opens
4. To execute the tests locally, select the **Run All Tests Locally** check box.

5. To execute the tests remotely, clear **the Run All Tests Locally** check box. For each test, you must select a host machine. Click the Run on Host grid box, and click the browse button. The Select Host dialog box opens. Under <Any Host>, you can select a host to run the test.

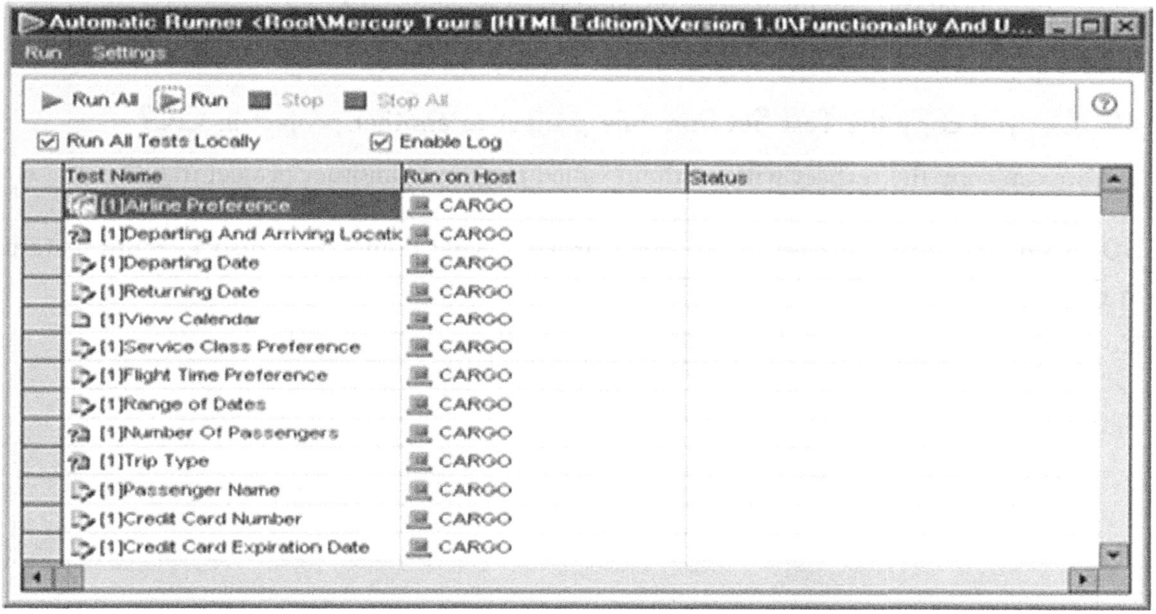

45. Can you change the test script status in Execution Grid?

No, We can't modify the status in the Execution Grid

46. How can you change the script status manually in the Execution Grid?

1. Double click on the test script instance in the Execution Grid
2. Test Runs (or Test Instance Properties) dialog opens
3. Modify the top most run status in the dialog box

47. How to view the Test Script's last run results in QC?

1. Select the script instance in the Execution Grid
2. Click Launch Report button to view the results

48. How to view the results for the previous runs of the script in QC?

1. Double click on the test script instance in the Execution Grid
2. Test Runs (or Test Instance Properties) dialog opens
3. Select the test run for which you want to view the results
4. Click Launch Report button

49. Can you copy the Test Set from one project to another project in QC?

Yes, we can copy the test set with/without called tests in to another project in QC

50. If you copy the test set in the same project, what could be scripts execution status in the copied test set?

No Run, scripts test runs and status can't be copied when you copy the test set

CHAPTER 23

Hybrid Automation Framework

A STEP-BY-STEP GUIDE FOR UNDERSTANDING AND IMPLEMENTATION

CHAPTER 23A

Overview of Automation Frameworks

Why Automation Framework?

The inclination to get automated testing activity is understandable,

- As automation test takes less time to run than manual test and gradually runs unattended.
- Automated tests enable to execute large volume of the tests, hence increases the coverage both by running more test cases and with many input data values.
- By freeing manual testers from having to execute repetitive tests, test automation enables them to focus on using their creativity.
- All the above advantages also helps in drastically reducing the costs

Goals of Automation Framework

The main goals for any good automation framework are,

- Re-usability
- Modularity
- Scalability
- Ease of deployment
- Portability

RECORD/PLAYBACK MYTH

The test automation tool vendors market their product as the main feature of the tool is the ability to capture the user actions and later to playback them. The basic drawback in this method is the scripts resulting from this method contain hard-coded values which must change if anything at all changes in our AUT. The costs associated with maintaining such scripts are very high and unacceptable. These scripts are not reliable, even if the application has not changed, and often fail on replay (pop-up windows, messages, and other things can happen that did not happen when the test was recorded). So, avoid using "Record/Playback" as a method of automation testing.

The record/playback feature of the test tool is useful for determining how the tool is trying to process or interact with the application under test, and can give us some ideas about how to develop your test scripts, but beyond that, its usefulness ends quickly.

TYPES OF TEST AUTOMATION FRAMEWORKS

As we have eliminated Record/Playback method, let us explore about the existing automation methodologies. There are several test automation frameworks available, among these the selection is made based on the factors such as reusability, modularity, user friendliness. The different test automation frameworks available are as follows,

- Test Script Modularity
- Test Library Architecture
- Data-Driven Testing
- Keyword-Driven or Table-Driven Testing
- Hybrid Test Automation

Test Script Modularity

The test script modularity framework is the most basic of the frameworks. The test script modularity framework requires the creation of small, independent scripts that represent modules, sections, and functions of the application-under-test. These small scripts are then used in a hierarchical fashion to construct larger tests, realizing a particular test case. The use of this framework will yield a higher degree of modularization and add to the overall maintainability of the test scripts.

Test Library Architecture

The test library architecture framework is very similar to the test script modularity framework and offers the same advantages, but it divides the application-under-test into procedures and functions instead of scripts. This framework requires the creation of library files (vbs,qfl) that contains functions to perform automation testing on the application-under-test. These functions in the library files are then called directly from the test script. Like Test Script Modularity framework this framework also yields a high degree of modularization and adds to the overall maintainability of the tests.

Data-Driven Testing

A data-driven framework is where test script is executed with various sets of test data read from data files (Datatable, ODBC sources, CVS files, Excel files, DAO objects, ADO objects, and such). In this framework Test Script to perform actions on the application-under-test has to be coded using the language supported by the automation tool (For Example VBScript for QTP). This Test Script also logs the test status to the Results file.

Merits of data-driven testing

The merits of the Data-Driven test automation framework are as follows,

- Application-Under-Test can be tested with various sets of Test Data.
- Scripts are an assembly of function calls
- Data for test cases read in from external source (e.g., Excel spreadsheet, ODBC database)
- Results can be captured externally per script execution (i.e., spreadsheet, database)

Demerits of data-driven testing

- Requires proficiency in the Scripting language used by the tool

Keyword-Driven Testing

This requires the development of data tables and keywords, independent of the test automation tool used to execute them and the test script code that "drives" the application-under-test and the data. Keyword-driven tests look very similar to manual test cases. In a keyword-driven approach for each test the functionality of the application-under-test is documented in a excel file as step-by-step instructions. In this method, the entire process is data-driven, including functionality.

For example the Login test case for yahoo contains actions like

1. Enter Login Name
2. Enter Password
3. Click Login button
4. Check Inbox page displayed.

The keyword table for the above test requirement will be as follows:

Test Table for Yahoo Login

Object Name	Object Type	Action	Input Value
		OpenURL	http://mail.yahoo.com
MailHome		setBrowserPage	
Login	WebEdit	Enter	DemoUser
Password	WebEdit	Enter	Demo123
Login	WebButton	Click	
MailInbox	Page	ObjExist	True

Results of execution are outputted to HTML and also to any other format like CSV using Results API.

Advantages:

- Proficiency in the Scripting language used by the tool is not necessary, hence a person without programming expertise can also involve in automation.
- Can be easily ported from one automation tool to another since Test Scripts will remain same irrespective of tool.

Disadvantages:

- Designing of Core Automation Framework requires extensive experience and effective programming skills.
- Making changes to framework is always a challenging activity since any mistake leads into failure of many Test Scripts.
- Development of Application-Specific Functions and Utilities requires proficiency in the tool's Scripting language.

Hybrid Test Automation Framework

Hybrid Test Automation Framework is a combination of all of the above techniques, pulling from their strengths and trying to mitigate their weaknesses. This hybrid test automation framework is what most frameworks evolve into overtime. Hybrid Test Automation Framework generally accommodates both Keyword-Driven as well as Data-Driven.

Our test automation framework is a Hybrid Test Automation Framework

CHAPTER 23B

Hybrid Framework Architecture

Hybrid Test Automation Framework is a combination of all of the above techniques, pulling from their strengths and trying to mitigate their weaknesses. This hybrid test automation framework is what most frameworks evolve into overtime. Hybrid Test Automation Framework generally accommodates both Keyword-Driven as well as Data-Driven.

Our test automation framework is a Hybrid Test Automation Framework

HYBRID FRAMEWORK BENEFITS

1	**Reusability**	The Hybrid Framework is an application-independent framework. Test Scripts and developed in Excel Sheets can be Re-used in Multiple Applications. For Example Login and Registration Test Scripts developed for one application can be used in other applications with minimal or no changes. Similarly Core Framework developed can be Re-Used for all applications without any modifications.
2	**Less effort**	The effort involved in coding and reviewing is minimal when compared to other frameworks since a good percentage of coding is done within the framework. The tester simply has to enter the keywords, reducing the time required for coding. Maintenance of the scripts is also easy.

3	**Control on Test Execution**	Test Scripts can be executed in a controlled manner where user can configure which Test Scenarios to Execute, which Test Scripts to Execute from the entire list of available Test Scenarios and Test Scripts.
4	**Increased quality**	The scripts will be of uniform quality since they make use of the same code.
5	**No scripting skills required by the end user**	No coding skills required to automate and to review the scripts. The scripts are user friendly with good readability. Scripts can be interpreted easily by a person who does not have complete knowledge of the tool and Scripting
6	**Return on investment is high**	Although the initial effort for building framework is high, in the long run, the return on investment will be high because of the reusability.

ARCHITECTURE OF A HYBRID FRAMEWORK

Architecture forms the foundation of any automation frame work. It should be robust enough to handle the desired functions efficiently and effectively. Our Hybrid Automation Framework Architecture comprises of two parts; Core Framework Layer and Application Layer.

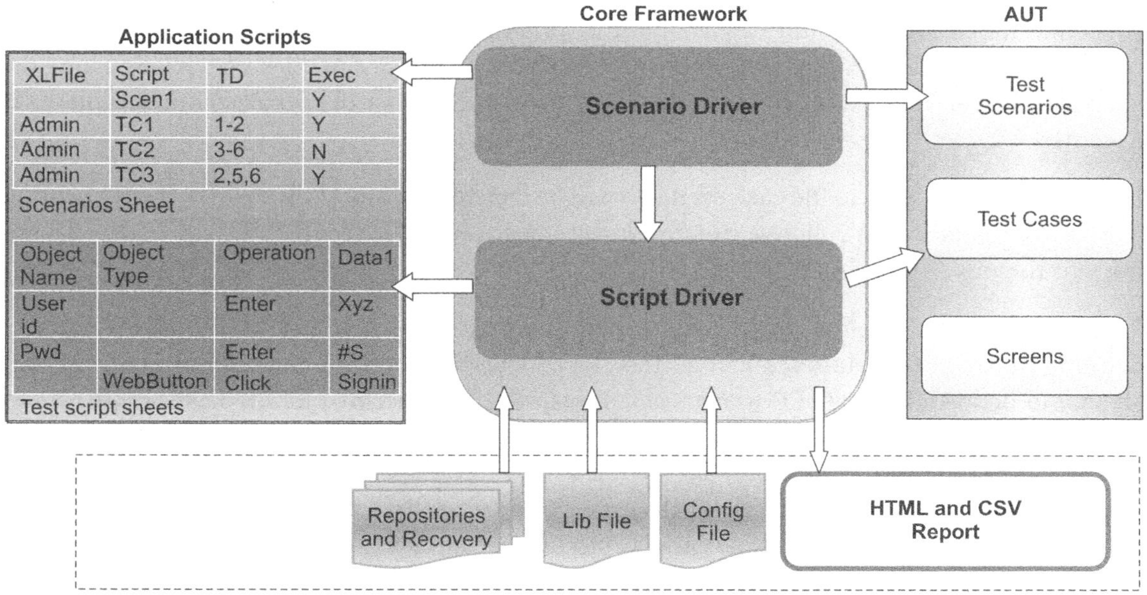

Hybrid Framework Architecture Diagram

Core Framework Layer

The Core Framework Layer is independent to any application and can be reused for automation of every web based application. Core Framework Layer consists of the following components that can be reused across all Applications:

- Scenario Driver
- Script Driver
- Keyword Functions
- Report Library

Application Layer

The Application Layer consists of the following components that have to be filled with Keywords and Test Data based on the testcases to be automated for a given application:

- Config File
- Scenario File
- Script Files
- Object Repository Files
- Recovery Files

Framework starts its execution by calling the scenario driver. Scenario Driver loads Library Files like Report Library and Keyword Functions Library. This also loads Config file which contains information Path of the repositories, Path of the Script files etc. Apart from this Scenario Driver also loads scenario file which contains the list of scenarios and scripts to be executed.

From the loaded scenario file each scenario will be considered one after the other for execution. If execution status is Y, then scripts under scenario will be executed. Else Scenario Driver goes to the next scenario.

The best part in our frame work is you can even control which test scripts to be executed by defining the execution status as Y or N. If script execution status is Y then corresponding script sheet will be loaded into QTP to run each step in the Test Script File. In Test Script File we will find Many columns like Step, Object Name, Object Type, Operation, TD_1,TD_2,TD_3 etc. Columns TD_1,TD_2 represent the Test data to be used in the Test Script. One more excellent feature about our frame work is we can even control the test data to be used while script is executing. User can specify the Test Data columns to be used in scenario file against the Test Script in the column TestData. User can specify each test data column to be used or he can also specify the Range of Columns to be used.

Corresponding to each keyword written in the test script we can find the Keyword functions in a Library File WebKeywords. Script driver calls these Keyword Functions and performs the operation on the object. Before we perform operation on the object of any page we will set the page to be used with the function **setBrowserPage**. This function also loads the repository corresponding to the page since Page name is same as object repository name. Other words we maintain one repository for each page.

While framework is executing status of each script execution will be logged to an HTML file which is stored in the results folder. Our results file is very detailed which contains Scenario name, test cases executed for each scenario, description of test step executed, Results of the test step PASS/FAIL. Results summary will also be stored in the CSV file along with detailed HTML report.

Folder Structure

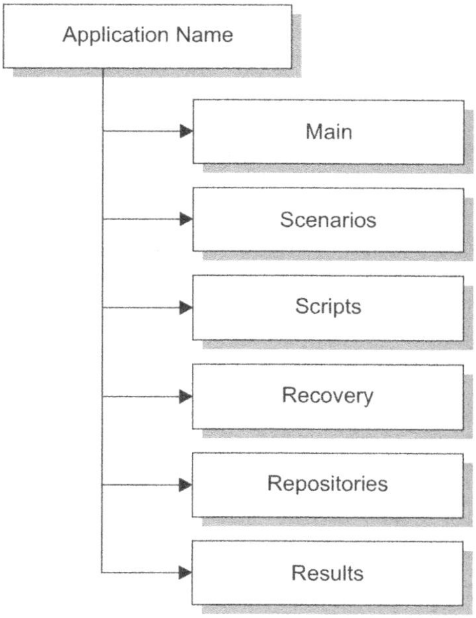

WALKTHROUGH OF FILES USED IN THE HYBRID FRAMEWORK

Below is the list of all files, functions used in the frame work and their purpose

File	Function	Description
Scenarios\ScenarioDriver		This QTP Script Starts scripts execution by calling ScenarioDriver function presented in Main\WebMainLib.vbs
Main\WebMainLib.vbs		This library file contains functions to Run the Scenario and Test Script.
	ScenarioDriver	Executes all the scenarios mentioned in the scenario file. Calls ScriptDriver for each TestScript in the given scenario.
	ScriptDriver	Runs each Testscript present in the scenario file. Calls Functions presented in Main\WebKeywords.vbs, based on the Keywords given by the user for performing a particular action on the AUT.
Main\WebKeywords.vbs		Contains Functions like OpenURL, SetBrowserPage which performs operations based on the script written by the user.
Main\ReportLib.vbs		Contains functions to create HTML report
	ReportScript	To report script name and description to HTML report
	CreateReport	To create HTML report File
	ReportResult	To report test cases or step result (PASS/FAIL) to HTML report

FLOW DIAGRAM

Below is the Flow Diagram of Framework Execution

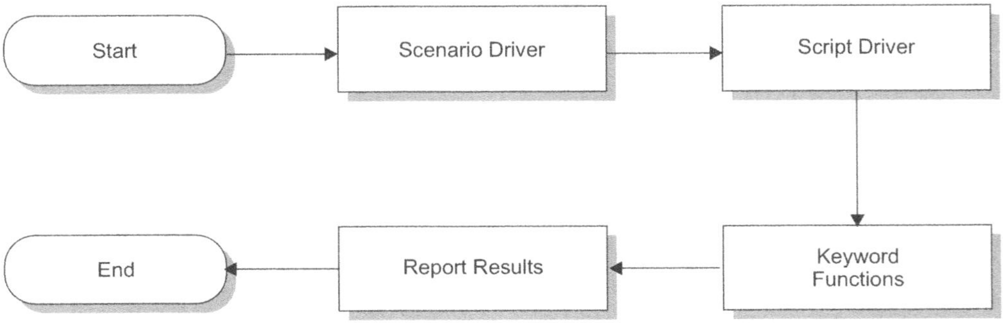

CHAPTER 23C

Using Keyword Functions

USING KEYWORD FUNCTIONS

To use Hybrid framework for any application we must understand the Keywords and their usage.

General usage rules of Keyword functions are

1. If keyword function is used by only one object then we need not to write ObjectType. Framework automatically takes care of it.

ObjectName	ObjectType	Operation	TD_1	TD_2
Country		SelectList	India	USA

2. If Keyword Function is used by multiple Object Types and it doesn't require any input TestData then use Test Data column to input object name as shown below:

ObjectName	ObjectType	Operation	TD_1	TD_2
	Link	Click	Advanced Search	Programming

3. If Keyword Function is used by multiple Object Types and require any input TestData then use Test Data column to input Test Data and ObjectName column to enter

ObjectName. If Test Data contains multiple values separate each value with comma (,)

ObjectName	ObjectType	Operation	TD_1	TD_2
search	WebButton	CheckProp	disabled,0	Height,0

Below are some of the commonly used Keyword Functions and their usage in the Test Script Sheets.

OpenURL

Purpose: To open specified URL of the web application

Example 1

ObjectName	ObjectType	Operation	TD_1	TD_2
		OpenURL	http://localhost/bookstore/Default.jsp	

- Opens Bookstore Home Page

Example 2

bjectName	ObjectType	Operation	TD_1	TD_2
		OpenURL	http://mail.yahoo.com	http://www.yahoo.com

- Opens Yahoo Mail Home Page while using Test Data 1 (TD_1)
- Opens Yahoo Home Page while using Test Data 2 (TD_2)

SetBrowserPage

Purpose: To load object repository corresponding to the page on which we are going to perform operations like clicking a button, Entering text into an Edit box, Clicking a Link etc.

Example 1:

ObjectName	ObjectType	Operation	TD_1
BSHome		setBrowserPage	

- Loads repository of Name *BSHome.tsr*
- This means further steps we are going to write in the Test Script Sheet will work on the objects stored in the repository *BSHome.tsr*

Example 2:

Opens Yahoo Mail Home Page

ObjectName	ObjectType	Operation	TD_1
BSAdmin		setBrowserPage	

- ➢ Loads repository of Name *BSAdmin.tsr*
- ➢ This means further steps we are going to write in the Test Script Sheet will work on the objects stored in the repository *BSAdmin.tsr*

CloseBrowser

Purpose: To close the opened browser.

Example 1:

ObjectName	ObjectType	Operation	TD_1
		CloseBrowser	

- ➢ Closes the Browser which is already opened.

Click

Purpose: To click on object represented by Image, Link, WebButton, WebElement

Example 1:

ObjectName	ObjectType	Operation	TD_1	TD_2
	WebButton	Click	Login	

- ➢ Clicks WebButton Named Login

Example 2:

ObjectName	ObjectType	Operation	TD_1	TD_2
	Link	Click	Advanced Search	Programming

- ➢ Clicks Link Named *Advanced Search* while using Test Data 1 (TD_1)
- ➢ Clicks Link Named *Programming* while using Test Data 2 (TD_2)

Example 3:

ObjectName	ObjectType	Operation	TD_1	TD_2
	Image	Click	Home	Logo

- ➢ Clicks Image Named *Home* while using Test Data 1 (TD_1)
- ➢ Clicks Image Named *Logo* while using Test Data 2 (TD_2)

SetCheckBox

Purpose: To select or unselect check box.

Example:

ObjectName	ObjectType	Operation	TD_1	TD_2
Send Product Updates		SetCheckBox	ON	OFF

- ➢ Sets check box Send Product Updates to ON while using Test Data 1 (TD_1)
- ➢ Sets check box Send Product Updates to OFF while using Test Data 2 (TD_2)

SelectList

Purpose: To select an item from drop down list

Example 1:

ObjectName	ObjectType	Operation	TD_1	TD_2
Country		SelectList	India	USA

- ➢ Selects *India* from Country list box while using Test Data 1 (TD_1)
- ➢ Selects *USA* from Country list box while using Test Data 2 (TD_2)

Example 2:

ObjectName	ObjectType	Operation	TD_1	TD_2
Country		SelectList	2	4

- ➢ Selects *2nd Item* from Country list box while using Test Data 1 (TD_1)
- ➢ Selects *4th Item* from Country list box while using Test Data 2 (TD_2)

Example 3:

ObjectName	ObjectType	Operation	TD_1	TD_2
Country		SelectList	"#2"	"#4"

- Selects 2nd *Item* from Country list box while using Test Data 1 (TD_1)
- Selects 4th *Item* from Country list box while using Test Data 2 (TD_2)

Enter

Purpose: To enter data in to text box.

Example:

ObjectName	ObjectType	Operation	TD_1	TD_2
AuthorName		Enter	Siva	

- Enters Siva in the AuthorName Edit box while using Test Data 1 (TD_1)

Example 2:

ObjectName	ObjectType	Operation	TD_1	TD_2
AuthorName		Enter	Prasad	Sudhakar

- Enters Prasad in the AuthorName Edit box while using Test Data 1 (TD_1)
- Enters Sudhakar in the AuthorName Edit box while using Test Data 2 (TD_2)

ObjExist( )

Purpose: To check object exists or not.

Example 1:

ObjectName	ObjectType	Operation	TD_1	TD_2
Home	Page	ObjExist	20	40

- Checks whether Page *Home* is displayed in the Browser. Waits for 20 sec during TD_1 and 40 secs during TD_2

Example 2:

ObjectName	ObjectType	Operation	TD_1	TD_2
Advanced Search	Link	ObjExist	30	50

- Checks whether link *Advanced Search* exists in the current Page. Current page is the page which was set by setBrowserPage in the previous statements.

Example 3:

ObjectName	ObjectType	Operation	TD_1	TD_2
Search	WebButton	ObjExist	20	20

- Checks whether Button *Search* exists in the current Page. Current page is the page which was set by setBrowserPage in the previous statements.

SelectRadioOption

Purpose: To select radio option

Example 1:

ObjectName	ObjectType	Operation	TD_1	TD_2
Gender		SelectRadioOption	Male	Female

- Selects Gender *Male* while using Test Data 1 (TD_1)
- Selects Gender *Female* while using Test Data 2 (TD_2)

Example 2:

ObjectName	ObjectType	Operation	TD_1	TD_2
Gender		SelectRadioOption	1	2

- Selects 1st *Item* from Gender Radio Group while using Test Data 1 (TD_1)
- Selects 2nd *Item* from Gender Radio Group while using Test Data 2 (TD_2)

Example 3:

ObjectName	ObjectType	Operation	TD_1	TD_2
Gender		SelectRadioOption	"#1"	"#2"

- Selects *1st Item* from Gender Radio Group while using Test Data 1 (TD_1)
- Selects 2nd *Item* from Gender Radio Group while using Test Data 2 (TD_2)

CheckProp

Purpose: Checks whether a property value of an object is equivalent to expected value.

Example 1:

ObjectName	ObjectType	Operation	TD_1	TD_2
Confirm Message	WebElement	CheckProp	innertext, Creation successful	innertext, Product addition failed

- Checks whether WebElement *Confirm Message* contains innertext property value as *Creation successful* while using Test Data 1 (TD_1).
- Checks whether WebElement *Confirm Message* contains innertext property value as *Product addition failed* while using Test Data 2 (TD_2)

Example 2:

ObjectName	ObjectType	Operation	TD_1	TD_2
search	WebButton	CheckProp	disabled,1	disabled,0

- Checks whether WebButton *search* contains disabled property value as *1* while using Test Data 1 (TD_1)
- Checks whether WebButton *search* contains disabled property value as *0* while using Test Data 2 (TD_2)

ClickDialogButton

Purpose: Clicks Button displayed on the Pop-Up Dialog

Example 1:

ObjectName	ObjectType	Operation	TD_1	TD_2
Confirm Delete		ClickDialogButton	OK	Cancel

- Clicks WebButton *OK* displayed on the Pop-Up dialog *Confirm Delete* while using Test Data 1 (TD_1)

➢ Clicks WebButton *Cancel* displayed on the Pop-Up dialog *Confirm Delete* while using Test Data 2 (TD_2)

1. Identify Mistakes in below code

Step	ObjectName	ObjectType	Operation	TD_1
1	http://localhost/bookstore/Login.jsp		OpenURL	
2			SetBrowserPage	,
3	Logo_bookstore		ObjExist	20
4	Login	WebEdit	Enter	admin
5	password		Enter	admin
6	Login	WebButton	Click	

Step 1: For OpenURL URL name must be provided under TD_1

Step	ObjectName	ObjectType	Operation	TD_1
1			OpenURL	http://localhost/bookstore/Login.jsp

Step 2: SetBrowserPage must have repository name to be loaded under ObjectName

Step	ObjectName	ObjectType	Operation	TD_1
2	SignIn		SetBrowserPage	,

Step 3: ObjExist must have ObjectType to be filled and also maximum timeout to be filled under Test Data. For ObjExist Keyword function ObjectType is mandatory since ObjExist can be used on variety of objects like WebButton, WebEdit, Image, Link etc. If we do not specify ObjectType then framework cannot understand on which type of the object you are applying the function ObjExist.

Step	ObjectName	ObjectType	Operation	TD_1
3	Logo_bookstore	Image	ObjExist	20

Step 4: ObjectType is optional since Keyword Enter works only on Text box. So Automation Framework automatically considers it as WebEdit box. Hence we can write correct code as below.

Step	ObjectName	ObjectType	Operation	TD_1
4	Login		Enter	admin

Step 6: Click method must have the button name to click in Test Data Sections. Correct Code is as shown below

Step	ObjectName	ObjectType	Operation	TD_1
6		WebButton	Enter	Login

1. Write a Test Script to login with username admin and password admin for the Login screen shown below.

Step	ObjectName	ObjectType	Operation	TD_1
1			OpenURL	http://localhost:8081/bookstore/Login.jsp
2	SignIn		SetBrowserPage	,
3	Enter login and password	WebElement	ObjExist	20
4	Login		Enter	admin
5	password		Enter	admin
6		WebButton	Click	Login
7	Administration Panel		SetBrowserPage	,
8	User Information	WebElement	ObjExist	20
9		Image	Click	icon_admin

2. Write a Test Script to insert the users Siva and Sudhakar in the MemberInsert page shown below

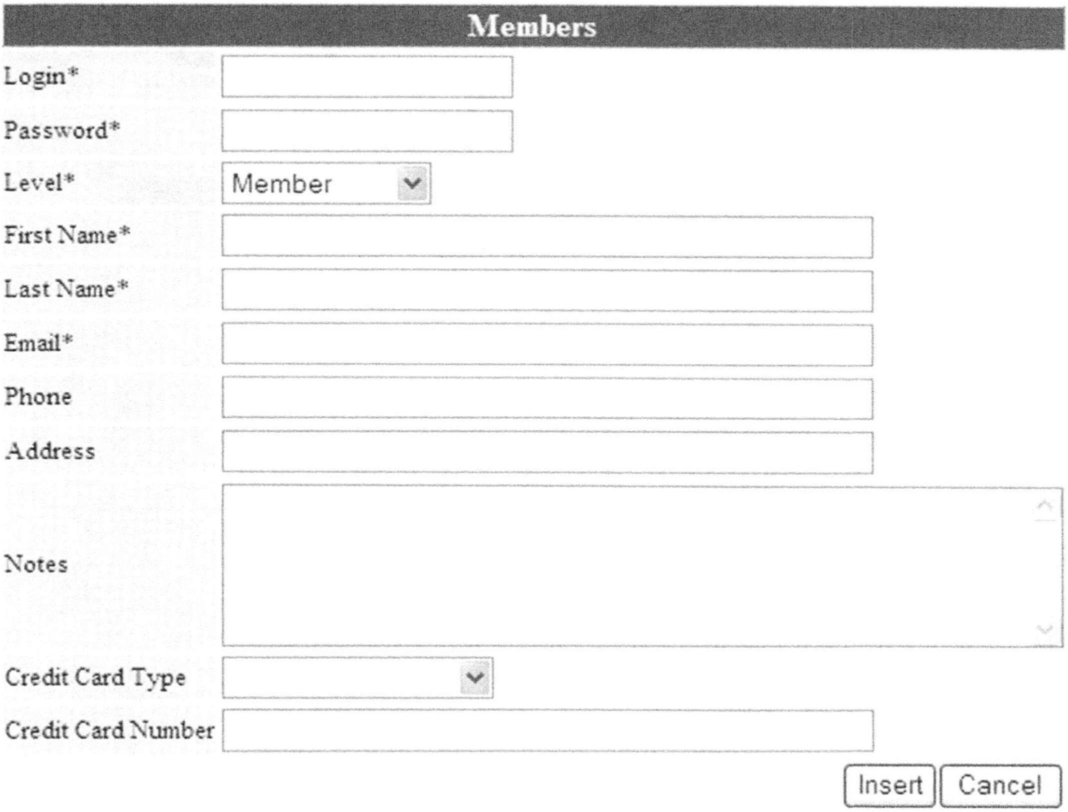

Step	ObjectName	ObjectType	Operation	TD_1	TD_2	
1.		MemberInsert		SetBrowserPage	,	,
2.	8	Members	WebElement	ObjExist	20	20
3.	9	Login		Enter	Siva	Sudhakar
4.	10	password		Enter	iibc!23	Iibc_123
5.	11	Level		SelectList	Member	Administrator
6.	12	FirstName		Enter	Siva	Sudhakar
7.	13	LastName		Enter	Reddy	Kakunuri
8.	14	Email		Enter	siva@yahoo.com	sudhakar@gmail.com
9.	15		WebButton	Click	Insert	Insert

3. Write a Test to Insert Book Details in the page shown below

CHAPTER 23D

Using Scenario File

Scenario file contains list of Test Scenarios to be executed. Below is the explanation of columns in scenario file and their usage.

XLFILE – Name of the Excel File that contains the Test Scripts to be executed. This value is NULL for row corresponding to Test Scenario.

SCRIPT – Name of the Test Script to be executed. Each Test Script is a sheet in an Excel file and the sheet contains the Keywords corresponding to the test case to be automated.

TESTDATA – Contains the details of Test Data to be considered for each Test Script Execution.

EXEC – Contains Y or N; indicating whether test script is to be executed or not.

```
Scripts1.xls contains TC1001,TC1002, TC1003, TC3003, TC2002

Scripts2.xls contains TC2001, TC3001,TC3002
```

4. Write a Scenario File for following

- **Scenario TS1 contains TestScripts TC1001,TC1002, TC1003**
- **Scenario TS2 contains TestScripts TC2001,TC2002**
- **Scenario TS3 contains TestScripts TC3001,TC3002, TC3003, TC1002, TC2001**

XLFILE	SCRIPT	TESTDATA	EXEC	Status
	TS1			
Scripts1	TC1001			
Scripts1	TC1002			
Scripts1	TC1003			
	TS2			
Scripts2	TC2001			
Scripts1	TC2002			
	TS3			
Scripts2	TC3001			
Scripts2	TC3002			
Scripts1	TC3003			
Scripts1	TC1002			
Scripts2	TC2001			

5. From the Above Run scenarios TS1 and TS3 and in TS3 run only TC3002, TC3003

XLFILE	SCRIPT	TESTDATA	EXEC	Status
	TS1			
Scripts1	TC1001	1		
Scripts1	TC1002	1		
Scripts1	TC1003	1		
	TS2			
Scripts2	TC2001	1		
Scripts1	TC2002	1		
	TS3		Y	
Scripts2	TC3001	1	N	
Scripts2	TC3002	1	Y	
Scripts1	TC3003	1	Y	

Scripts1	TC1002	1	N	
Scripts2	TC2001	1	N	

6. From the Above

a. Run TC1002 for Test Data columns2,3,4

b. Run TC3002 for Test Data columns2,7,9

c. Run TC1003 for Test Data columns 1 to 3,6,8

XLFILE	SCRIPT	TESTDATA	EXEC	Status
	TS1			
Scripts1	TC1001	1		
Scripts1	TC1002	2-4		
Scripts1	TC1003	1-3,6,8		
	TS2			
Scripts2	TC2001	1		
Scripts1	TC2002	1		
	TS3			
Scripts2	TC3001	1		
Scripts2	TC3002	2,7,9		
Scripts1	TC3003	1		
Scripts1	TC1002	2-4		
Scripts2	TC2001	1		

7. Write a Scenario File for following

Test Scenario Name: TS5

Scripts and Runs:

TC3001 : 1-3,7,4

TC2002: 1,4,8

TC3003: 7,6,5

Test Scenario Name: TS6
Scripts and Runs:

TC1003 : 4,6
TC2002: 1,2,3
TC3002: 4,6,7,8

Test Scenario Name: TS7
Scripts and Runs:

TC1001 : 1,2
TC2001: 2,3
TC3003: 6,7,8

CHAPTER 23E

Scenario Driver

Scenario Driver is a function that executes all the scenarios mentioned in the scenario file. Script Driver reads each row in scenario file and decides whether to execute scenario and script. If it has to execute script, then it loads script sheet and calls script driver.

1. Import Config sheet from Config.xls into Config Sheet of Datatable

```
ConFile = "D:\IIBCHAF\Config.xls"

'Configuration file

Datatable.AddSheet "Config"

Datatable.ImportSheet ConFile,"Config","Config"
```

2. Read Scenarios file path from Config sheet

```
ScenariosFile = Datatable("ScenariosFile","Config")
```

3. Import Scenarios sheet from Scenarios file into Scenarios Sheet of Datatable

```
Datatable.AddSheet "Scenarios"

Datatable.ImportSheet ScenariosFile,"Scenarios","Scenarios"
```

4. Read Results path from Config sheet and Create Results folder with Current Date

```
ResPath = Datatable("ResultsPath","Config")
```

```
ResFolderPath = ResPath & "\" & MonthName(Month(Date)) & Day(Date) & " "
& Year(Date)

CreateResultsFolder(ResFolderPath)
```

5. Create a loop to run from first Row to Last row of scenarios sheet and Read values of columns XLFILE and EXEC

```
For r =1 to  Datatable.GetSheet("Scenarios").GetRowCount

Datatable.GetSheet("Scenarios").SetCurrentRow r

      ScrFile = Datatable("XLFILE","Scenarios")

      Execs = Datatable("EXEC","Scenarios")
```

6. If XLFILE value is NULL and EXEC value is N this means we should not execute scenario. So write a code that sets next row to read is Next Scenario. Note that next scenario is identified by NULL value of XLFILE column

```
If ScrFile = "" AND Execs="N" Then

      Do

            r = r+1

            Datatable.GetSheet("Scenarios").SetCurrentRow r

            ScrFile = Datatable("XLFILE","Scenarios")

            If ScrFile = ""  Then

                  r = r-1

                  Exit Do

            End If

      Loop

End If
```

7. If XLFILE value is NULL and EXEC value is Y this means we should execute scenario. Create HTML report file for this scenario.

```
If ScrFile = "" AND Execs="Y" Then          'Scenario
      ScrStatus = "Passed"
```

```
        Scenario = Datatable("SCRIPT","Scenarios")

        ResFile = ResFolder &  "\" & "_" & Scenario & "_" &  Day(Date)& "-" &
        Month(Date) & "-" & Year(Date) & "-" & Hour(Time) & "-" & Minute(Time)
        & "_Res.html"

        Datatable("ResFile","Config")=ResFile

        CreateReport ResFile,Scenario

End IF
```

8. If XLFILE value is Not NULL and EXEC value is Y, this means we should execute current Test Script.

- ➢ Check whether previous script is Passed or Failed. If passed, then only run the next scripts.
- ➢ Read Script Sheet name from SCRIPT column.
- ➢ Call Script Driver with Script Excel File Name, Script Sheet Name and TestData
- ➢ Report the Test Script Execution status Pass and Fail to **Status** column of Scenario Sheet

```
If ScrFile <> "" AND Execs="Y" Then

      If  ScrStatus = "Passed" Then 'Check Previous Script Status

            ScrFile=Datatable("ScriptsPath","Config") &"\"&ScrFile&".xls"

            ScrSht = Datatable("SCRIPT","Scenarios") 'Test Case Name

            TcRuns = Datatable("TESTDATA","Scenarios") 'Test Case Data Runs

                  ScrStatus = ScriptDriver(ScrFile,ScrSht,TcRuns) 'Call
                  ScriptDriver

            If ScrStatus  = "Passed" Then
                  Datatable("Status","Scenarios") = "Passed"

             Else

                  Datatable("Status","Scenarios") = "Failed"

            End if

      End If

End If
```

CHAPTER 23F

Implementing Script Driver

Scenario Driver calls Script Driver for each TestScript the Script Driver is supposed to execute. Scenario Driver passes three arguments to Script Driver; Name of the Excel Sheet where Test Script is present, Name of the Test Script and Test Data to be used. Steps Performed by Script Driver are:

1. Import Script Sheet to Datatable

```
Datatable.AddSheet ScrSht

Datatable.ImportSheet ScrFile,ScrSht,ScrSht
```

2. Loop Test Script execution for each Test Data

```
DataRun = SplitTestData(TcRuns)

For dn = 0 To ubound(DataRun) 'For Each TestData
```

Note: SplitTestData is a function that takes TestData String as input and returns an array containing each array element as a Test Data column number.

3. Loop for each keyword in the Test Script File and read the values of columns ObjectName, ObjectType, Operation and Test Data. These values are used to create a Keyword Function.

```
For i = 2 to Datatable.GetSheet(ScrSht).getRowCount 'Steps Loop in the Script
```

```
    Datatable.GetSheet(ScrSht).setCurrentRow i
    StepNo = Datatable("Step",ScrSht)
    Obj = Datatable("ObjectName",ScrSht)
          Operation = datatable("Operation",ScrSht) 'Operation or Keyword
    Ipval = datatable(Td,ScrSht)
    cls=datatable("ObjectType",ScrSht)
```

4. If Operation is SetBrowserPage then assign store Page Name in a variable which is used during Keyword function Creation. Also note that Page Name and Browser Name are always same.

```
If  Operation = "SetBrowserPage" Then
          pname=Obj
End If
```

5. Create and Call Keyword Function

```
Func =  Operation&"  pname,Obj,cls,Ipval,StepDes"
Execute Func 'Execute Keyword Function
```

6. Report Function Execution Status to Results File. If Result is Failure Stop Executing the Test Script for further steps and Test Data

```
If Err.Description <>"" Then  'Error in Script Driver
      TcStatus = "Failed"
      Exit For
End If
```

7. Delete Test Script Sheet from Data Table and return result to Scenario Driver

```
Datatable.DeleteSheet ScrSht
ScriptDriver = TcStatus
```

CHAPTER 23G

Implementing Keyword Functions

Now let us understand how to implement Keyword Functions. For an effective implementation of keyword function, first we must have clear idea of whether this Keyword function is used by one type object or multiple types of objects. For Example *Enter* is a Keyword Function which is used by One Type of Object called Text Box. Whereas *Click* is a Keyword Function used by Multiple Types of Objects like WebButton, Link, Image. We must also have a clear idea whether Keyword Function Takes Input Data or Not. For Example Keyword function Enter requires value to be entered as Input, whereas Keyword function Click does not require any Input.

Using the above information we will plan how the columns ObjectName, ObjectType, TestData to be filled in the Test Script Sheet.

GENERAL IMPLEMENTATION GUIDELINES

1. Every Keyword Function should have following syntax

```
Public Function KeywordFunctionName (pname,Obj,cls,Ipval, stepDes)
```

Pname – Page Name. This is also Browser Name

Obj – Object Name

Cls – Object Class like Link,Image,WebEdit,WebButton

Ipval – Input Value

StepDes – Step Number

2. Input Parameters must be used appropriately based on the usage of Keyword Function. For Example for a click method Ipval is the Name of the Object and for Enter method Input value is the Text to be entered.

3. Every Keyword Function Report Execution Result using ReportResult function which has following syntax:

```
ReportResult stepDes, TcStatus,TcExpRes,TcActRes
```

StepDes – Step Number

TcStatus – Keyword Function Passed/ Failed

TcExpRes – Expected Operation of Keyword Function

TcActRes - Actual Operation performed by Keyword function.

Refer Chapter: Report Library for Detailed explanation of the function

Implementing *Enter* Function

Purpose of this function is to enter text in the edit box

Usage:

ObjectName	ObjectType	Operation	TD_1	TD_2
AuthorName		Enter	Siva	

From the above usage, we can understand that Object Name is in Object Name column. So the Object Name of Web Edit box is stored in the input parameter *Obj* and Text to be entered is stored in the input parameter *Ipval.* Always page name and object names are represented by variable pname. Also observe that we do not need ObjectType because this function is always used on WebEdit. Hence variable *cls* automatically represents WebEdit. So the line to enter text in the edit box is:

```
Browser(pname).Page(pname).WebEdit(Obj).Set Ipval
```

Complete code for **Enter** Keyword Function is as follows

```
Public Function Enter(pname,Obj,cls,Ipval, stepDes)
```

```
On Error Resume Next

Err.Clear

'Enter Value in the Edit box

Browser(pname).Page(pname).WebEdit(Obj).Set Ipval

'Formulate Expected output text string which will be shown in HTML results file

TcExpRes = "Enter "&  Ipval &" in " & Obj & " text box"&"<BR>"

'Check Any Error while setting value in Edit box

'Formulate Actual output text string which will be shown in HTML results file

If Err.Description <>"" Then

      TcStatus = "Failed"

 TcActRes = "Application Error: " & "Enter: " & Err.Description

Else

      TcStatus = "Passed"

      TcActRes="Entered "&  Ipval &" in " & Obj & " text box"&"<BR>"

End If

    ReportResult StepDes,TcStatus,TcExpRes,TcActRes

End Function
```

TcExpRes variable should always be coded to reflect the meaning of the operation performed in this function. Since the above function represents enter operation in the text box we have written the code as below:

```
TcExpRes = "Enter "&  Ipval &" in " & Obj & " text box"&"<BR>"
```

In the above example *Obj* value AuthorName and *Ipval* is Siva *TcExpRes* variable will contain following text

```
TcExpRes ="Enter "&" Siva"&" in"&" AuthorName"& "text box"
```

Net meaning of above is

```
TcExpRes ="Enter Siva in AuthorName text box"
```

Similarly *TcActRes* also should be coded to reflect PASS or FAIL result of the Keyword function executed.

Implementing *SelectList* Function

Purpose of this function is to select an item from list box

Usage Example:

ObjectName	ObjectType	Operation	TD_1	TD_2
Country		SelectList	India	USA

From the above usage we can understand that Object Name is in Object Name column. So the Object Name of Web Edit box is stored in the input parameter *Obj* and *item* to be selected is stored in the input parameter *Ipval.* Always page name and object names are represented by variable pname. Also observe that we do not need ObjectType because this function is always used on WebList. Hence variable *cls* automatically represents List. So the line to select item in the list box is:

```
Browser(pname).Page(pname).WebList(Obj).Select Ipval
```

Complete code for **SelectList** Keyword Function is as follows

```
Public Function SelectList(pname,Obj,cls,Ipval, stepDes)

On Error Resume Next

Err.Clear

      Browser(pname).Page(pname).WebList(Obj).Select Ipval

      TcExpRes = "Select "&  Ipval &" from " & Obj & " List box"&"<BR>"

      If Err.Description <>"" Then

            TcStatus = "Failed"

                  TcActRes = "Application Error: " & "SelectList: " &
Err.Description

      Else

                  TcStatus = "Passed"

                  TcActRes="Selected "&  Ipval &" from " & Obj & " List
box "&"<BR>"
```

```
        End If

    ReportResult StepDes,TcStatus,TcExpRes,TcActRes

End Function
```

Implementing *Click* Function

Purpose is to click on any given object.

Usage Example:

ObjectName	ObjectType	Operation	TD_1	TD_2
	Link	Click	Advanced Search	Programming

From the above usage we can understand that Object Name is in Test Data column. So the Object Name of Link is stored in the input parameter *Ipval*. Also observe that we entered ObjectType because this function is used by multiple object types. Hence variable *cls* contains the ObjectType. So the line to click the link is:

```
Browser(pname).Page(pname).Link(Ipval).click
```

Please note that object name for Link is *Ipval* variable.

Since the same Keyword Function is used for multiple Object types we will use Select Case to select the object type and perform the operation.

Complete code for **Click** Keyword Function is as follows

```
Public Function Click(pname,Obj,cls,Ipval, stepDes)

   On Error Resume Next

   Err.clear

      Select Case cls

            Case "Link"

                  Browser(pname).Page(pname).Link(Ipval).click

            Case "Image"

                  Browser(pname).Page(pname).Image(Ipval).click

            Case "WebButton"

                  Browser(pname).Page(pname).WebButton(Ipval).click
```

```
            Case "WebElement"
                  Browser(pname).Page(pname).WebElement(Ipval).click
            End Select
      TcExpRes = "Should Click "&  Ipval & " " & cls & "<BR>"
      If Err.Description <>"" Then
            TcStatus = "Failed"
 TcActRes = "Application Error: " & "Click:  " & Err.Description
      Else
            TcStatus = "Passed"
            TcActRes="Clicked "&  Ipval & " " & cls & "<BR>"
         End If
      ReportResult StepDes,TcStatus,TcExpRes,TcActRes
End Function
```

Implementing Own Keyword Function — DblClick

Now Let us write a new Keyword Function DblClick which is not available in Framework. Purpose of this function is it should DblClick the objects of Type Link, Image and WebButton.

Usage Example1:

ObjectName	ObjectType	Operation	TD_1	TD_2
	Link	DblClick	Advanced Search	Programming

Usage Example2:

ObjectName	ObjectType	Operation	TD_1	TD_2
	WebButton	DblClick	Search	

From the above usage we can understand that Object Name is in Test Data column. So the Object Name of Link is stored in the input parameter *Ipval.* Also observe that we entered ObjectType because this function is used by multiple object types. Hence variable *cls* contains the ObjectType. So the line to click the link is:

```
Browser(pname).Page(pname).Link(Ipval).FireEvent "ondblclick"
```

Complete code for **DblClick** Keyword Function is as follows

```
Public Function Click(pname,Obj,cls,Ipval, ByRef stepDes)
   On Error Resume Next
   Err.clear
Select Case cls
Case "Link"
           Browser(pname).Page(pname).Link(Ipval).FireEvent
"ondblclick"                       Case "Image"
           Browser(pname).Page(pname).Image(Ipval).FireEvent
"ondblclick"
Case "WebButton"
           Browser(pname).Page(pname).WebButton(Ipval).FireEvent
"ondblclick"               End Select


TcExpRes = "Should Dobule Click "&  Ipval & " " & cls & "<BR>"
      If Err.Description <>"" Then
            TcStatus = "Failed"
 TcActRes = "Application Error: " & "Click:  " & Err.Description
      Else
            TcStatus = "Passed"
            TcActRes="Double Clicked "&  Ipval & " " & cls & "<BR>"
         End If
      ReportResult StepDes,TcStatus,TcExpRes,TcActRes
End Function
```

EXERCISES

1. Design and Implement Keyword Function CheckRowCount for web table. This function should be used to check whether Row Count in the web table is correct or not?
2. Design and Implement Keyword Function myEnter for WebEdit to enter text into textbox.
3. Design and Implement Keyword Function myClick to click objects WebButton, Image, Link.

CHAPTER 23H

Report Library

Report Library is used to report Test execution status to HTML Report File. Creating HTML Report file is very easy since it is nothing but writing HTML tags into a text file to create a Results file. To create a good HTML results file knowledge of HTML TAGS is very essential. We recommend the user to refresh their HTML skills before reading this chapter. HTML Results file in our Hybrid frame appears as shown below.

Test Case / Scenario)	Expected Result	Actual Result	Status
BookStore Login-TD_1::PS0100-1_BookStoreLogin	12:57:32 PM		
	Logo_bookstore should be displayed	Logo_bookstore is displayed.	Passed
	User Information should be displayed	User Infomation is displayed.	Passed
Insert Member-TD_1::PS0100-1_Insert members	12:57:40 PM		
	Administration Menu should be displayed	Administration Menu is displayed.	Passed
	Members should be displayed	Members is displayed.	Passed
	Members should be displayed	Members is displayed.	Passed
	Members should be displayed	Members is displayed.	Passed

Report Library contains 4 functions as follows

- ➢ CreateResultsFolder
- ➢ CreateReport
- ➢ Report Script
- ➢ ReportResult

CreateResultsFolder

This function creates a results Folder to store Results. Steps performed by this function are very simple.

- Check Folder Exists.
- If Not Create Folder

```
If Not fso.FolderExists(fldrPath) Then
      fso.CreateFolder(fldrPath)
End If
```

CreateReport

This function creates Results File in the Results Folder and also adds header. Header looks as shown below

Test Case/Scenario	Expected Result	Actual Result	Status

Steps performed by this function are

1. Open Results file in Append mode. Create if the file doesn't exist

```
Set fso = CreateObject("Scripting.FileSystemObject")
Set Myfile = fso.OpenTextFile(ResFile,8,True)
```

2. Create header as a table cells. Table Width is 950 which is divided into 4 cells 45%,24%,24%,7%

   45% - Test Case Name

   24% - Expected Result

   24% - Actual Result

   7% - Status (Pass/Fail)

```
Myfile.Writeline("<table width=" & "950" & " border=" & "1" & " cellpadding=" & "1" & " cellspacing=" & "0" & ">")

Myfile.Writeline("<tr>")

Myfile.Writeline("<td width=" & "45%" & "><font style="&"""COLOR: green; FONT-FAMILY: 'Times New Roman'"""&"size="&"3"&"> <b> Test Case / Scenario) </b></font></td>")
```

```
Myfile.Writeline(“<td width=” & “24%” & “><font style=”&”””COLOR: green; FONT-FAMILY: ‘Times New Roman’”””&”size=”&”3”&”> <b> Expected Result </b></font></td>”)

Myfile.Writeline(“<td width=” & “24%” & “><font style=”&”””COLOR: green; FONT-FAMILY: ‘Times New Roman’”””&”size=”&”3”&”> <b> Actual Result </b></font></td>”)

Myfile.Writeline(“<td width=” & “7%” & “><font style=”&”””COLOR: green; FONT-FAMILY: ‘Times New Roman’”””&”size=”&”3”&”> <b> Status </b></font></td>”)

Myfile.Writeline(“</tr>”)

Myfile.Writeline(“</table>”)
```

Report Script

This function is used to report Test Script Name to Results File. Test Script Name appears in results file as shown below.

BookStore Login-TD_1::PS0100-1_BookStore Login	12:57:32 PM

Code is similar to above except that table row contains only 2 cells and Table width is divided for 2 Cells as 45%,55%

45% - Test Script Name

55% - Execution Time

Code snippet for creating table row in HTML Results File is

```
Set Myfile = fso.OpenTextFile(Datatable(“ResFile”,”Config”),8,True)

Myfile.Writeline(“<table” & “ width=” & “950” & “ border=” & “1” & “ cellpadding=” & “1” & “ cellspacing=” & “0” & “>”)

Myfile.Writeline(“<tr>”)

Myfile.Writeline(“<td width=” & “45%” & “><font style=”&”””COLOR:” & color & “ ; FONT-FAMILY: ‘Times New Roman’”””&”size=”&”2”&”> <b>” & ScriptName & “</b></font></td>”)

Myfile.Writeline(“<td width=” & “55%” & “><font style=”&”””COLOR:” & color & “ ; FONT-FAMILY: ‘Times New Roman’”””&”size=”&”2”&”> <b>” & ExecTime & “</b></font></td>”)
```

```
Myfile.Writeline("</tr>")

Myfile.Writeline("</table>")
```

ReportResult

This is the function used to report execution status of each Step/Keyword Function in the results file. If Keyword Function execution Passes status color is GREEN, else both status and actual result colors are RED. Step Execution Report is as shown below.

InsertMember-ID_2::icon_admin	12:57:44 PM		
	Administration Menu should be displayed	Administration Menu is displayed	Passed
	Step 4 - Enter admin	Application Erro: Enter Failed to run the test due to an unknown error.	Failed

Code is similar to above. Variables storing information to write step/Keyword Function execution status in Table cells are

er – Expected Result

ar – Actual result

status – Execution Status (Pass/Failed)

1. If Status is Passed report result in GREEN color

```
Myfile.Writeline("<td width =" & "24%" & "><font style="&"""COLOR: black; FONT-FAMILY: 'Times New Roman'"""&"size="&"2"&"> " & er & "</font></td>")

Myfile.Writeline("<td width=" & "24%" & "><font style="&"""COLOR: black; FONT-FAMILY: 'Times New Roman'"""&"size="&"2"&"> " & ar & "</font></td>")

Myfile.Writeline("<td width=" & "7%" & "><font style="&"""COLOR: green; FONT-FAMILY: 'Times New Roman'"""&"size="&"2"&"> <b>" & status & "</b></font></td>")
```

2. If Status is Failed report Result in RED color

```
Myfile.Writeline("<td width =" & "24%" & "><font style="&"""COLOR: black; FONT-FAMILY: 'Times New Roman'"""&"size="&"2"&"> " & er & "</font></td>")
```

```
Myfile.Writeline("<td width=" & "24%" & "><font style="&"""COLOR: red; FONT-FAMILY: 'Times New Roman'"""&"size="&"2"&"> " & ar & "</font></td>")

Myfile.Writeline("<td width=" & "7%" & "><font style="&"""COLOR: red; FONT-FAMILY: 'Times New Roman'"""&"size="&"2"&"> <b>" & status & "</b></font></td>")

End If
```

CHAPTER 23I

Framework Interview Questions

1. Which framework do you follow?

We follow Hybrid Test Automation framework.

2. Why do you call your framework as Hybrid Test Automation framework?

Our framework uses most important features of automation like Modularity, Keyword Driven and Data Driven. This frame work completely eliminates script writing. We can specify keywords in the Test Script File and each keyword is equal to one operation to be performed on the application object. Since we are writing keywords in the excel file this framework is called as Keyword driven framework. This frame work also has a facility to Data Drive the Test Script by specifying multiple sets of Test Data.

3. Explain the Architecture of your frame work

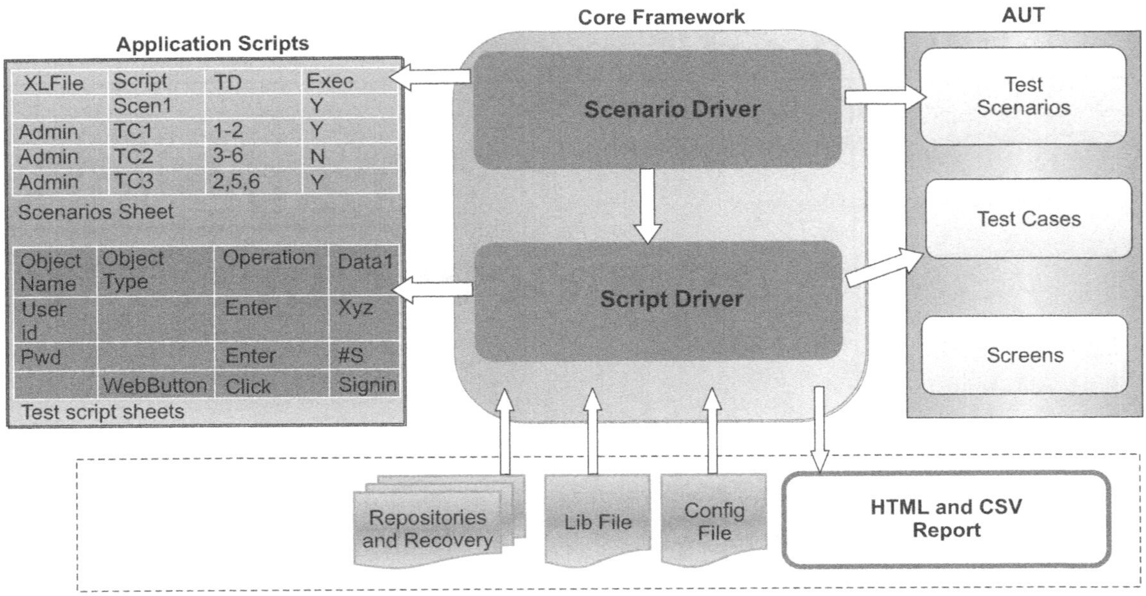

Hybrid Framework Architecture Diagram

Core Framework Layer

The Core Framework Layer is independent to any application and can be reused for automation of every web based application. Core Framework Layer consists of the following components that can be re-used across all Applications:

- Scenario Driver
- Script Driver
- Keyword Functions
- Report Library

Application Layer

The Application Layer consists of the following components that have to be filled with Keywords and Test Data based on the testcases to be automated for a given application:

- Config File
- Scenario File
- Script Files

- ➢ Object Repository Files
- ➢ Recovery Files

Framework starts its execution by calling the scenario driver. Scenario Driver loads Library Files like Report Library and Keyword Functions Library. This also loads Config file which contains information Path of the repositories, Path of the Script files etc. Apart from this Scenario Driver also loads scenario file which contains the list of scenarios and scripts to be executed.

From the loaded scenario file each scenario will be considered one after the other for execution. If execution status is Y then scripts under scenario will be executed. Else Scenario Driver goes to the next scenario.

The best part in our frame work is you can even control which test scripts to be executed by defining the execution status as Y or N. If script execution status is Y then corresponding script sheet will be loaded into QTP to run each step in the Test Script File. In Test Script File we will find Many columns like Step, ObjectName, ObjectType, Operation, TD_1,TD_2,TD_3 etc. Columns TD_1,TD_2 represent the Testdata to be used in the Test Script. Onemore excellent feature about our frame work is we can even control the test data to be used while script is executing. User can specify the Test Data columns to be used in scenario file against the Test Script in the column TestData. User can specify each test data column to be used or he can also specify the Range of Columns to be used.

Corresponding to each keyword written in the test script we can find the Keyword functions in a Library File WebKeywords. Script driver calls these Keyword Functions and performs the operation on the object. Before we perform operation on the object of any page we will set the page to be used with the function **setBrowserPage**. This function also loads the repository corresponding to the page since Page name is same as object repository name. Other words we maintain one repository for each page.

While framework is executing, the status of each script execution will be logged to an HTML file which is stored in the results folder. Our results file is very detailed which contains Scenario name, test cases executed for each scenario, description of test step executed, Results of the test step PASS/FAIL. Results summary will also be stored in the CSV file along with detailed HTML report.

4. Advantages of your frame work

- ➢ No scripting skills required by the end user
- ➢ Consistent and Good Quality

- Effective Control on Test Case Execution
- Reusability
- High ROI (Return on Investment)
- Easy Maintenance
- Effective results reporting

5. Features of your framework

- Keyword Driven
- Data Driven
- Easy To Understand and Use
- Re-usability
- Effective control on Test case Execution

6. How do you say No Scripting Skills are required to work with your frame work?

Anyone who wants to automate a Test Case using our framework needs to know the keyword functions and their purpose. By entering these keywords in specific order user can create a Test script to perform the steps mentioned in the Test Case with various sets of Test Data.

7. Without Scripting Skills how do you manage your framework?

For managing framework like maintaining Script Driver, Scenario Driver and also for creating Keyword Functions, knowledge of scripting is essential. However for using the Keyword Functions and creating automated Test Scripts end user need not to have any scripting skills.

8. How can you say your frame work is easy to Understand and Use?

The way we created Keyword Functions is most of them are self explanatory from their name itself. Hence anyone can easily understand and use them to automate the test case.

9. What is your contribution to framework

I was involved in writing some of the keyword functions, writing the script driver which calls these functions. I have also been involved in creating Reports Library.

10. Name Few Important Keywords in your Framework.

SetBrowserPage

OpenURL

ObjExists

Click

Enter

SelectList

SelectRadio

11. How do you control the execution of Test scenarios and Testcases?

In Scenario File I can enter Y or N in the column EXEC. If I doesn't want a Test Scenario to be executed I keep N in EXEC column adjacent to Test Scenario. Similarly if I doesn't want test case to be executed I keep N in EXEC column adjacent to Test Case.

12. Where and how will you configure your test script to run for data present in Columns 2,6,8,9 and 15-25

- ➢ Open Scenario File
- ➢ Go to Row containing Test Script
- ➢ In the column Test Data enter 2,6,8,9,15-25

13. I want you to change the Test data for a particular test script. How will you achieve this?

- ➢ Open Excel File Containing Test Script
- ➢ Select sheet containing Test Script
- ➢ Wants to add new Test Data Create a Test Data column as TD_N(TD_5,TD_6)
- ➢ Wants to Change an existing Test Data go to corresponding Test Data column and modify values.

14. How will you see the execution summary of your test scripts?

- ➢ Go To Framework Results Folder
- ➢ Go To Test Execution Date Folder under Results Folder
- ➢ Open Excel file Scenarios.xls and observe the status column to see the execution status of each Test Script.

15. How will you see the detailed report on each testcase executed?

- Go To Framework Results Folder
- Go To Test Execution Date Folder under Results Folder
- Open HTML file corresponding to each Scenarios and go through the step by step execution status of the Test Script.

16. What does a configuration file contain?

Configuration File contains the path for Scenario File, Scripts File, Results Folder and Recovery Files.

17. Where do you specify the URL for an application?

Application URL has to be specified in OpenURL function.

18. If you are following Shared repository how will you deal with new objects which are not part of shared repository?

I will go ahead and add them to the shared repository using object repository manager. All I need to take care is I should not change logical names of existing objects. This is because other scripts using these objects might be affected.

19. Can you explain one critical requirement you automated and why you feel it is critical?

I was automating a Color selection from a color palette. Tool was not recognizing each color in color pallet as different object. I have used Keyboard Arrow Key and moved to a particular color and selected them. Initially it was a very difficult one to automate but finally we solved it with this technique.

Note: You must answer atleast one or two cases based on your project.

20. If I want you to create framework entirely from scratch can you do that?

Yes. I can.

21. What are is the difference between Global Functions and Business Functions?

Global functions are the Keyword Functions used in every project. Business Functions are the keyword functions used only in a specific project.

22. How will you design the framework for a given project?

I must consider various factors before designing the framework like Code Reusability, Easy Script Maintenance, Object repository Maintenance, Usage of Multiple sets of Test Data. Based on these factors I must come out with a framework that effectively handles all these issues.

23. How are the results stored in your Automation Framework?

Results of execution are stored in an HTML format and Excel file format.

24. How do you identify the errors if script doesn't execute correctly.

Our Results file report is a step by step based. So I can easily find out the error from results file and correct it. If problem requires even more detailed analysis I can run the scripts in debug mode and isolate the error.

25. Are you using configuration management to maintain the changes for your script? If not how do you track the changes?

If your answer is NO:
Unfortunately, we do not have any configuration management tool integrated with QC. However we take weekly backups by exporting each script in zip format. This backup data we refer in case we want to revert to previous versions of the script.

If your answer is YES:
Yes. We do use configuration management to maintain the changes to our script where each change is saved like a new version of the file.

26. What are the limitations of your framework?

I cannot call them as limitations but I can say few enhancements planned in our framework are

- A feature to enable and disable Recovery Scenarios on a need basis only for few steps. Right now Recovery Scenarios are enabled for whole execution.
- Support for descriptive programming within the frame work.
- Support for conditions like if, else. But this requirement is not very high priority considering the design of the framework.

Index

Made in the USA
Monee, IL
05 November 2026

67385494R00142